The Fun of Living Together

The Fun of Living Together

"We must learn to live together as brothers or perish together as fools."

—Martin Luther King, Jr.

Roberta Grimes *with* Kelley Glover

By the Author

Liberating Jesus

My Thomas

The Fun of Dying

The Fun of Staying in Touch

The Fun of Growing Forever

The Fun of Living Together

The Fun of Meeting Jesus
(Children's Picture-Book)

This book is dedicated to every child whose ancestors were held in American slavery. Dear beautiful lights of tomorrow, your time has come.

The Fun of Living Together

By: Roberta Grimes with Kelley Glover

Copyright © 2016, 2022 by Roberta Grimes

All rights reserved.

This book or part thereof may not be reproduced in any form, stored in a retrieval system, or transmitted in any form by any means—electronic, mechanical, photocopy, recording or otherwise—without prior written permission of the publisher, except as provided by United States of America copyright law. The text of the *New American Standard Bible*® may be quoted and/or reprinted up to and inclusive of one thousand (1,000) verses without *express written permission of The Lockman Foundation,* providing the verses do not amount to a complete book of the Bible nor do the verses quoted account for more than 50% of the total work in which they are quoted.
"Scripture quotations taken from the New American Standard Bible,
Copyright © 1960, 1962, 1963, 1968, 1971, 1972, 1973,
1975, 1977, 1995 by The Lockman Foundation
Used by permission." (www.Lockman.org)

Publisher's Cataloging-In-
Publication Data (Prepared by The
Donohue group, Inc.) Names:
Grimes, Roberta | Glover, Kelley.
Title: The fun of living together / by Roberta Grimes with Kelley Glover.
Description: Normal, IL, Greater Reality Publications |
Series: The fun of …; [4]
Identifiers: ISBN 978-1-7374107-0-6 (paperback) | ISBN 978-1-7374107-1-3 (ebook) Subject: LCSH: Race relations—Religious aspects—Christianity. | Discrimination—Religious aspects—Christianity. | United States—Race relations. | Slavery—United States—History. | Jesus Christ—Teachings.
Classification: LCC BT7374.2 G75 2017 (print) | LCC BT734.2 (ebook| DDC 261.8348-dc23

Published by

GR

Greater Reality Publications
PO Box 341
Normal, IL 61761

ISBN: 978-1-7374107-0-6
Printed in the United States of America
Cover picture and design credit: Ratha C. Grimes

Table of Contents

Foreword Three American Leaders i
Roberta's Introduction 1
Kelley's Introduction... 7

Understanding America's Most Intractable Problem

Chapter One: The Story of American Slavery Since Abolition 15
Chapter Two: Understanding and Overcoming Bigotry 29
Chapter Three: Imagining a Slavery-Free America 39
Chapter Four: A Stranger in a Strange Land 47

Building Our Bright Shared Future

Chapter Five: Why Separations Among People are Destructive 61
Chapter Six: Why Some Possible Remedies Never Will Work 67
Chapter Seven: Proposing Thomas Jefferson's Solution 73
Chapter Eight: Attacking Other Forms of Bigotry 87
Chapter Nine: The Crucial Role of Individual Action............................. 95
Chapter Ten: Envisioning a United Country and an Eternally Peaceful World 101

Appendices

Appendix I: Reading Suggestions 109
Appendix II: Kelley's Transformational Healing Tool 117
Appendix III: Roberta's Transformational Healing Tool 121
Appendix IV: What Would Jesus Really Do? 127

Foreword
Three American Leaders

The United States of America is suffering its deepest divisions since the Civil War. The causes of the discord in our society seem to be varied and complex, but your authors believe they come down to one core problem that will have to be addressed before anything much ever can improve, either in this nation or in the world. Bringing our country together is going to require every heart to the effort! And we are confident that it can be done if all of us will rally around three transformational American leaders.

Martin Luther King, Jr., was quoting Thomas Jefferson when he said in July of 1965:

'We hold these truths to be self-evident, that all men are created equal, that they are endowed by God, Creator, with certain inalienable rights, that among these are life, liberty and the pursuit of happiness.'

"This is a dream. It's a great dream.

"The first saying we notice in this dream is an amazing universalism. It doesn't say, 'some men'; it says 'all men.' It doesn't say 'all white men'; it says 'all men,' which includes black men. It does not say 'all Gentiles'; it says 'all men,' which includes Jews. It doesn't say 'all Protestants'; it says 'all men,' which includes Catholics. It doesn't even say 'all theists and believers'; it says 'all men,' which includes humanists and agnostics.

"Never before in the history of the world has a sociopolitical document expressed in such profound, eloquent and unequivocal language the dignity and the worth of human personality. The American dream reminds us—and we should think about it anew on this Independence Day—that every man is an heir of the legacy of dignity and worth."

Then on January 16, 2017, four days before his Inauguration, President Donald J. Trump took note of the holiday that bears Dr. King's name with these words:

"Today our nation pauses to honor a legend, an icon, and an American hero. The Reverend Dr. Martin Luther King Jr. lifted up the conscience of our nation—a towering leader in his day, and a lasting inspiration for all generations to follow.

"Our Declaration declares that 'all men are created equal,' and Dr. King challenged our nation to live out that sacred truth: to banish the evils of bigotry, segregation and oppression from the institutions of society and the hearts of men.

"His legacy of freedom is the true memorial to his life: no testimonial can pay better tribute than the faces of young children living out their dreams.

"But his work is not done: all around us today we see communities and schools falling behind and not sharing in the prosperity of American life. Each of us has a solemn obligation to ensure that no American is left behind—and that all Americans are fully included in the American Dream. When young Americans of color are left on the sidelines, our nation is denied a lifetime of contributions to this society—and when any of our American brothers and sisters is forced to live in fear, or poverty, or violence, it is setback for the entire nation.

"We rise and fall together, and today we pledge to follow in Dr. King's footsteps so that all Americans may know the full blessings of this God-blessed land."

President Trump's pledge is a challenge to us all that ties back to Dr. King's civil rights struggle and then farther back, to the universal promises of freedom and equality of opportunity that were made at this nation's founding. President Trump has vowed to make the American dream attainable for every young descendant of slavery, and in doing that he will need all our help.

If not us, who? If not now, when?

Roberta's Introduction

Roberta Grimes

"We hold these truths to be self-evident: that all men are created equal; that they are endowed by their Creator with certain unalienable rights; that among these are life, liberty, and the pursuit of happiness."

— From the Declaration of Independence, Thomas Jefferson, 3rd president of the United States (1743–1826),

"The assertion that 'all men are created equal' was of no practical use in effecting our separation from Great Britain and it was placed in the Declaration not for that, but for future use."

— Abraham Lincoln, 16th president of the United States (1809–1865)

"Tonight, we gather to affirm the greatness of our nation—not because of the height of our skyscrapers, or the power of our military, or the size of our economy. Our pride is based on a very simple premise, summed up in a Declaration made over two hundred years ago."

— Barack Obama, 44th president of the United States

"Our scientific power has outrun our spiritual power. We have guided missiles and misguided men."

— Martin Luther King, Jr., Winner of the 1964 Nobel Peace Prize (1929–1968)

"There is nothing wrong with America that cannot be cured by what is right with America."

— Bill Clinton, 42nd president of the United States

"I like thinking big. If you're going to be thinking anything, you might as well think big."

— Donald Trump, 45th president of the United States

S*ome two hundred and forty years after it declared itself an independent nation, the United States of America still remains the world's best hope.*

American presidents as varied as Thomas Jefferson and Abraham Lincoln, Ronald Reagan and Barack Obama have reminded us that this country is meant to be a beacon of freedom and an example to the world of good government that protects the rights and nurtures the ambitions of every American. Yet the United States at the start of the twenty-first century is a sadly divided and bummed-out nation. It is able to offer little hope for the future even of its own people, and it seems inadequate to the task of doing much for the rest of the world.

Every thoughtful American can see wounds and fissures in most areas of our civic life, but few realize how many of these issues are the fruit of one overriding problem that has plagued this country from its founding. Repeatedly we have thrown money at what seemed to be fixes for America's first sin. We have framed laws to kill it and declared it dead, but zombielike it blunders on. After federal spending greater than the national debt and the blighting of millions of children's lives, in truth we have made no progress at all in putting the burden of slavery behind us.

So it is time now, once and forever, to fix this core American problem. And I say this with some urgency. Those that we used to think were dead are telling us that unless we can arrest the negative course of the United States we face a worldwide decline into barbarism. What alarms me is that the beginnings of the chaotic events these elevated beings predict already are plain to see! Exotic diseases and declining birthrates; universal hatred and mistrust; religious strife and the concentration of power and wealth in the hands of just a few: carry forward present trends, and the desolate hell that those that we used to think were dead now tell us soon will overspread the earth can be readily foreseen. Also, poignantly, a perfect alternative future occasionally can be glimpsed in small, hopeful flames that flicker to life but soon die to embers. Either future is possible. But at the moment, the worst case is ascendant.

Those of us living in the United States can look at the troubling trends beginning, and at the responsibility to start to fix the world that apparently we now face, and we can simply shrug and do nothing. It is going to take awhile for disease, famine, violence and chaos to turn out all the lights, so America likely will hold together until after you and I are dead. In the face of overwhelming odds against us, of course it is tempting to pass the buck; but unfortunately for me, I love my grandchildren. I am stuck with a desperate need to solve this problem, and to solve it right away!

One of the advantages of being old is that having seen many decades of history can give you some perspective. I remember the happy nineteen-fifties, the chaos of the sixties and seventies, the robust and hopeful eighties and nineties. And I can see now as I look back at my life how most of our problems are knitted together and derive from one gigantic mistake that was made at this nation's founding. We planted the tree of liberty without first clearing away one prominent rock, and by now that rock has caused the tree to grow in ever more twisted ways as it struggles to remain precariously upright and tries to find enough soil to be nurtured. That destructive rock is slavery. We have spent the past two hundred and forty years busily building the United States, repeatedly giving slavery a little attention to try to make it go away. But it hasn't gone away. It is time to accept the fact that it won't go away on its own. I submit to you that until we dig that rock from among this nation's roots and finally, definitively haul it away, it will continue to unbalance the country upon whose stability and growth the whole world depends. And inevitably, if that rock remains, this American experiment in personal freedom and self-governance is going to weaken. The tree of liberty will destabilize and fall. And it could take civilization with it.

I understand that what I am saying may seem preposterous to you. Not only am I listening to dead people, but I am saying now that slavery still exists as America's core problem? This may seem lunatic to you at first blush, and I get that. But for the sake of your grandchildren, for the sake of your country and the world, for the sake of all that matters to you, I ask you please to be still for a moment and let me make my case.

Actually, this won't be just my case. A close friend of mine is melanin-enriched, and when I told her I was planning to write this book she offered to help me do it. Kelley Glover's life is the embodiment of what every American of color can enjoy once we finally fix this problem. She is a music teacher and an entrepreneur, the daughter of a retired college president, two generations into the upper middle class. I love her because she is wise and funny and she understands me as perhaps no one else does, so when she offered to help me write this book and

keep me from making a fool of myself I invited her to be its co-author. We have chosen to make it a part of my Fun series and to write it in my voice, but every part of this book is Kelley's work as much as it is my own.

For most of my life I have been whitebread-clueless about the problems faced by African-Americans. I have loved the words of Martin Luther King, Jr., but like most of us who are melanin-deficient, I have assumed that the battles that he fought had been won. It is only with Kelley's help that I see that the terrible effects of American slavery are as much an immediate and desperate issue as they were a hundred and fifty years ago. I look now at little dark-skinned children, beautiful and bright and with eyes full of dreams, and I vow that their lives are going to be lived entirely beyond slavery's stain. We are going to fix this now, for every child of every race.

To make our success at ending slavery possible, we emphatically ask that you not assign blame. Blaming people will just make our problems worse! Please assume that everything done until now was the fruit of well-meant efforts by people of kindness and good will, and work with us to understand the present well enough that we can fix the future. Please forgive the past altogether! If we don't do that, all our efforts will be useless. And if you wish that Kelley and I had said something differently in some spot, had mentioned something that we have left out, or just had not written this book at all, then we ask that you forgive us as well.

And because minced-words silliness is the current weapon that is being ineffectively tried against slavery, we are not going to be politically correct here. To be perfectly frank, words are not our problem! All the many times in a century and a half that we have condemned and destroyed people for using the word "nigger" have done nothing whatsoever to change the condition of descendants of America's chattel slaves, so to hell with it now. ***Who cares what we say? All that will matter from this day forward will be what you and I will do.***

Kelley's Introduction

Kelley Glover

"I refuse to accept the view that mankind is so tragically bound to the starless midnight of racism and war that the bright daybreak of peace and brotherhood can never become a reality . . . I believe that unarmed truth and unconditional love will have the final word."
—Martin Luther King, Jr.,
winner of the 1964 Nobel Peace Prize (1929–1968)

"You'll make mistakes. Some people will call them failures but I have learned that failure is really God's way of saying, 'Excuse me, you're moving in the wrong direction.'"
—Oprah Winfrey,
American media entrepreneur and talk show host

"If you don't like something, change it. If you can't change it, change your attitude."
—Maya Angelou,
American poet and civil rights activist (1928–2014)

"I will not have my life narrowed down. I will not bow down to somebody else's whim or to someone else's ignorance."
—bell hooks, American author and social activist

"It may be true that the law cannot make a man love me, but it can keep him from lynching me, and I think that's pretty important."
—Martin Luther King, Jr.,
winner of the 1964 Nobel Peace Prize (1929–1968)

"Nothing is more powerful than an idea whose time has come."
—Victor Hugo, French poet, novelist, and dramatist
(1802–1885)

I am so tired! And I'm tired of being tired! I know we have to be careful about how we make "I am" statements, but, you know what? *That* is part of the problem. When humans have a strong *belief* about something, it becomes a part of our *being*. Beliefs affect our thoughts, and those thoughts become a part of our bodies. Why do you think African-Americans have such a high rate of heart disease, high blood pressure, and diabetes? I've read that 47% of American Blacks have high blood pressure, as opposed to 27% of White Americans. Melanin-enriched Americans *feel* tired and *think* we're tired. This racism, prejudice thing becomes an "I am" statement in our minds and bodies, and that energy affects everyone else because, guess what, people? We really are all one: black, brown, white, yellow, and red. We are all in this together, whether we want to realize it or not! We are only as strong as our weakest link, so **"We must learn to live together as brothers or perish together as fools."** Martin Luther King has been right all along. It's time that we finally listen to him!

So, why am I tired, you ask? I can barely think of a time when the amount of melanin in my skin wasn't a major part of my awareness, or when my presence didn't make some people uncomfortable. I first became aware that my chocolate skin was seen as "less than" when I was four years old. We lived in an upper-middle-class Black neighborhood in Detroit, Michigan, and many of the people who lived around us were very light-skinned African-Americans. (There is a reason why this was true which I will explain later, since you may not be familiar with color and class within melanin-enriched communities in the U.S. and around the globe.)

My dear friend, who I will call Bobby, used to play with me in my front yard almost every day. Whenever the occasion arose for me to go inside my home to get something for us to play with, my friend Bobby would disappear from my yard and would not return for the rest of the day. Puzzled, I asked my mother why Bobby always disappeared and wouldn't come back, so she watched from inside to find out what was going on. Bobby's mother, who was a very fair-skinned, naturally red-headed Black woman with freckles, came over to our yard, grabbed his hand, and said to her little boy, "I told you I don't want you playing with that Black girl!" Translation: I don't want my light-skinned Black son being with a dark-skinned Black girl. Where does this mindset come from? Why did Bobby's mother not want her son to play with a darker shade of Black? S.L.A.V.E.R.Y. Vestiges of slavery. This is an example of what is called "colorism," or internalized racism, which I will delve into later in my own chapter of this book.

At age five I entered kindergarten, and I had my first experiences with outright, blatant racism from White children and White teachers. My parents actually sat me down at the age of five to tell me that some Black people are "color-struck," meaning they believe lighter skin is better than darker skin. Lighter skin means having more European ancestry, which makes a color-struck person feel as if their lighter shade is better than an individual with a darker shade. *And* they also told me that some people of European descent believed they were better than Black people, no matter their skin tone, because of something called racism. My parents had to have this difficult conversation with me because we were about to move from a mostly Black neighborhood in Detroit, Michigan, to a mostly White neighborhood in Mercer Island, Washington, an affluent suburb of Seattle.

Having to process that information at such a young age is a strange feeling. To believe you are awesome, and to learn that to others you are something less just because of the shade of your skin, is not an easy thing to live with day in and day out. However, I am so glad that my parents prepared me! The ways the kids reacted to me in my predominately White new school were interesting. Some kids approached me with curiosity, having never seen a Black person outside of television. Those classmates would ask me questions like, "Are you really White, and you just colored yourself with a brown crayon?" Or, "Why is your skin so dark? Did you get a sun tan?" Other kids were not as sweet in their curiosity. A few called me Blackie, nigger, or African. Back in the 1970's, at least in the Pacific Northwest and the Midwest, being called an African was a *huge* insult to a Black person, and being called *that* would often start physical fights, just as much as the N-word! *Ridiculous,* but true! *This* is why I have no problem with someone calling me African-American now. For so long there used to be so much *shame* associated with being of African descent. Later in this book we will talk about how the emotions of shame (namely Black and Brown people's shame) and guilt (namely White people's guilt) affect all Americans today. And how these patterns of insanity have stopped us from ever growing beyond discriminating against each other.

So, what did my parents tell me to call the kids who tried to shame me by calling me African? "If they call you African, which is accurate because that's where most of your ancestors are from, call them European if they are European-American, or Asian if they are Asian-American." Taking this approach helped these children who were being taught to hate to realize how *ridiculous* they were being. There was no shame in being European! There was no shame in being Asian, either. So, why would I be ashamed of being of African descent? It stopped them in their tracks *every* time! They would look shocked, think about it, and later on they'd ask me to play with them. Sometimes shock is the best medicine! Interrupting thought patterns helps to change belief systems permanently.

I am forty-eight years old. And yeah, I'm tired of dealing with this. However, I don't deal with it now in the same manner as I did at age six, or even at age twenty-five for that matter. I use spiritual tools to help me release things that have nothing to do with me. What other people think of me is really none of my business, so when racist things happen to me, I "go high" and soar even higher. I now view these kinds of negative experiences as opportunities to tap into my higher self and higher power, and I see them as only that. *Experiences!* I'm not saying that I never feel anger, hurt, resentments, etc., but I sure get over them faster now that I am older and wiser and have been dealing with these kinds of things for the past forty-four years! The spiritual tools I use transcend race, gender, religion, and sexuality, and can be used by all human beings who are trying to be kinder to themselves and to each other. It's time to finally get over ourselves so we can at last find "The Fun of Living Together."

That better world is still out there, ahead of us. And it still is not too late.

Understanding America's Most Intractable Problem

Chapter One
The Story of American Slavery Since Abolition

"Discrimination is a hellhound that gnaws at Negroes in every waking moment of their lives to remind them that the lie of their inferiority is accepted as truth in the society dominating them."
—Martin Luther King, Jr.,
winner of the 1964 Nobel Peace Prize (1929–1968)

"Our Declaration of Independence was held sacred by all and thought to include all; but now, to aid in making the bondage of the Negro universal and eternal, it is assailed, sneered at, construed, hawked at, and torn, till, if its framers could rise from their graves, they could not at all recognize it."
—Abraham Lincoln,
16th president of the United States (1809–1865)

"As long as you are black, and you're gonna be black till the day you die, no one's gonna call you by your goddamn name. So no matter what you are called, nigger, you just let it roll off your back like water, and you'll make it. Just pretend you're a goddamn piece of furniture."
—Lyndon Johnson,
36th president of the United States (1908–1973)

"Whatever someone did to you in the past has no power over the present. Only you give it power."
—Oprah Winfrey,
American media entrepreneur and talk show host

"I have decided to stick with love. Hate is too great a burden to bear."
—Martin Luther King, Jr.,
winner of the 1964 Nobel Peace Prize (1929–1968)

"We shall nobly save or meanly lose the last best hope of earth."
—Abraham Lincoln,
16th president of the United States (1809–1865)

I grew up in a little New England town where everyone was white. I was so far removed from racial tensions that two specific moments of my childhood stand out starkly in my mind. I recall that when I was six or seven I remarked to my mother that our family doctor looked exactly like Nat King Cole. Mom sputtered, "But he's black!" I said, "Except for that." And I was right. Except for skin shade, they could have been twins. Then later on, as a junior in college, I brought home my beloved to share our Thanksgiving turkey. He was tall, beautiful, gentle and sweet, and the smartest person I ever have known. It never dawned on me until my father first laid eyes on him that the fact that his parents were Chinese immigrants ever could matter to anyone.

I am to this day fundamentally clueless about America's most intractable problem. I cannot understand why racial or ethnic differences would matter to anyone! But they do indeed matter, and the fact that we cannot get beyond the racial and class issues that lie at the core of America's culture is destroying what Abraham Lincoln and others have called "the last best hope of earth." So your authors have tried to step back far enough to look at this matter objectively, and we have spotted what we are confident is the reason why our country is so broken. You may be surprised at our answer! But we cannot ever fix this problem until we first can understand it, so please hear us out. As astonishing as this thought may seem at first, most of America's current problems stem from the fact that to this day it never has entirely freed its slaves.

Coming to Grips with Slavery's Changing Face

A century and a half after the Civil War, America continues to grapple with slavery. It's as if the guns still echo, since the descendants of America's slaves remain by and large debased and dependent and relegated to the margins of American life. Oh, a few have done better. There are some black doctors and lawmakers now, black athletes and business folks and entertainers, but their individual successes do little to elevate the condition of so many others! Nearly half of America's black preschool-aged children live in poverty to this day, as compared with fewer than fifteen percent of young white children. Perhaps most appalling of all is the fact that at the start of the twenty-first century, while only thirteen percent of the American population is melanin-enriched, *blacks make up close to forty percent of the 2.2 million male inmates now being held in America's prisons*. Indeed, forty percent of black American men are in prison now or are ex-offenders, as compared with only fourteen percent of the white male population. For far too many men with darker skin, moving in and out of prison is a way of life.

This disastrous lack of progress by the descendants of American slaves is hard to fathom unless we examine our history since 1865. It is understandable that it might have taken a couple of generations for the freed slaves' descendants to assimilate into American life, and of course we know that for a time there were Jim Crow laws and separate-but-equal theories and other attempts to enforce segregation and to subjugate those with darker skin that ended as late as the nineteen-sixties. But even if we assume that the task of completing the emancipation of America's slaves has been ongoing for only the past fifty years, still we've got to say that when compared with the descendants of white immigrants, the descendants of slaves have made too little progress.

Take my own family. My grandparents were Danish immigrants who spoke little English and knew nothing but farming. Their children—my parents—made it through high school and became a bookkeeper and a secretary. Then I went to college and to law school. My children were born into the American dream. This is the way that it's supposed to be! And the fact that white immigrants to the United States routinely manage in two generations the kind of progress that most descendants of slavery still cannot dream of making even after a century and a half is a shame and a stain upon this earth.

In retrospect, it is hard to imagine how anyone could have thought the Civil War would end slavery. Slaves were descended from Africans who had been brought here against their will. They were treated like animals by their oppressors, marked by their skin shade as inferior, never educated and never encouraged to aspire to a future in the American mainstream. For the great mass of America's slaves, legal emancipation meant only that they were homeless and hopeless and living beneath the boot of everyone who was white. And to make matters worse, many of those white folks were extremely angry! Their region had just suffered a destructive invasion by their fellow Americans in what some southerners still refer to as the War of Northern Aggression. Little effort was made by anyone to help the mass of slaves to learn what freedom meant or how to behave as free Americans beyond some efforts made to get them to vote (whatever voting was). They were strangers in a strange land.

This book includes two quotations from President Lyndon Johnson that will make your hair stand on end. His racial attitude was typical of whites who grew up in the Jim Crow south, hearing tales of the Civil War and its aftermath from the perspective of its southern white victims. Imagine being a dark- skinned person surrounded by folks who thought as he did! But yet, Lyndon Johnson was instrumental in passing the Civil Rights Act of 1964 over the strong opposition of his fellow southern Democrats. Despite his history, he became a civil rights hero.

It is obvious the American Civil War did not end American slavery. Instead, our failure then to complete the emancipation process only relegated the descendants of America's slaves to a century of what amounted to slavery without papers, and eventually to an appalling re-enslavement by our benevolent federal government.

America's Botched Emancipation

Every slave held in the United States was legally freed by 1866, but still they remained in penury. Rather than stepping into their promised forty acres and a mule and being helped to learn to assume all the rights and opportunities of free Americans, the newly freed slaves simply joined the colored freedmen who for generations had been huddled at the base of American life. To have a dark complexion in the United States was then such a mark of inferiority that while some did manage to improve their station, for nearly all former slaves and their descendants the American dream of advancement still remained altogether beyond their grasp.

We must never forget that southern whites had suffered devastation during the Civil War at the hands of their fellow Americans. By their lights, they had a right to be enraged! The United States as they knew it then was a union of semi-independent nations, so they seem to have seen their Civil War defeat very much as Europeans today might see the use of the army of France by the government of the European Union to defeat and destroy all the rest of Europe in order to impose better-quality wine choices. Or if you would prefer an American analogy, it was to them as if today every so-called "red" state were to use the armed forces of the United States to conquer and destroy all the "blue" states in order to prevent their use of unisex bathrooms.

We are appalled now to imagine that anyone would think that slavery was a lifestyle option, but slavery had been a common practice since civilization began. For those living in the American south in the first half of the nineteenth century, slavery was no more disgusting than brutally imprisoning felons is to us today. And the melanin-deficient folks who lived in the nineteenth-century American south were proud of centuries of what seemed to them to have been a rich and glorious history.

In hindsight, it might have been better if the federal government and abolitionist groups had instead conducted an intensive program of re-education—okay, we'll call it propaganda—to enlighten southern folks about the evils of slavery. After all, in 1860 fewer than a third of white southerners owned slaves, and less than one percent of them owned more than 50 slaves. Were you aware of that fact? Not only did most southerners not own slaves, but many didn't even know a slaveholder. A nationwide anti-slavery propaganda campaign begun early in the nineteenth century could have led to a complete emancipation that would have included the compensation of slaveholders who were being deprived of what had been their legal property.

Compensating the slaveholders would have been expensive, but it could have prevented the brutal subjugation of the newly-freed slaves and their descendants that set in after the Civil War. And when compared with the cost of the Civil War, it would have been a bloody bargain! The estimated value of all the slaves in the Confederate states as of 1860 was just over two billion dollars, which is less than half of the more than six billion dollars that the north spent in fighting the Civil War. Add in the two billion dollars or so that the Confederate states spent on the losing side, and it is clear that for the federal government to have bought and freed every slave in America as part of a complete emancipation would have been much the better choice.

And then there is the fact that six hundred thousand Americans died in the Civil War, which is more than have died in all the other wars that we have fought, combined. Our attempt to end slavery by violent means was the most devastating war in American history, and yet even with the loss of so much blood and treasure it accomplished almost nothing. America so thoroughly botched emancipation by first tainting it with unthinkable violence and then ignoring the need to introduce the slaves to freedom and enlighten the public to accept these new Americans that even a hundred and fifty years later the evil that is slavery blunders on.

As you pause to consider how much better educating the public to accept a legal emancipation might have worked, think of the use of fur as clothing a hundred years later. In the fifties and sixties the rich still proudly wore their minks and sables. The rest of us envied them the wealth that let them do that, but few people thought what they were doing was evil. Now the idea of killing animals and wearing their skins is repulsive to many Americans, but that wasn't the case until fur activists began to work on changing the public's perceptions.

You ought to know, too, that one American Founding Father tried to end slavery at this nation's birth. There never has been a more ardent abolitionist than Thomas Jefferson was in his youth! Lincoln's insight that the first words of the second paragraph of the Declaration of Independence seemed to have been written as a plea to end slavery was entirely right. Then when Jefferson couldn't persuade his fellows to make ending slavery a founding American tenet, he developed a plan for ending slavery during his lifetime in a way that would have removed that rock from the roots of the tree of liberty and allowed it to grow straight and true. Unfortunately, events soon turned against him. We'll say more about this later.

The First Hundred Years of Post- Emancipation Slavery

Most American politicians living at the start of the nineteenth century seem to have seen slavery as something that was going to have to be addressed, only not quite yet. As had been true of the Revolutionary generation, they had more immediate things on their minds. So instead of using gentle propaganda to turn the minds of all Americans over the first half of the nineteenth century toward a peaceful emancipation by law that could have been almost universally supported, this country's solons let slavery fester until it threatened the breakup of the union. Then of course there came a war that humiliated and destroyed a large part of these United States.

Most of the whites who lived in the South lost family members and were rendered destitute by an invading army unleashed upon them by their fellow Americans. Then when the Civil War ended you could not easily spot the large planters and the politicians who arguably had brought it on, but the newly-freed slaves were easy to spot so those innocents bore all the white Southerners' fury. Not only were the mass of Southerners unable to assist the former slaves when they themselves had lost almost everything, but there rose in them an understandable but highly troublesome determination to keep the newly-freed slaves from taking any part of what little the South had left.

For a century, those with darker skins were kept debased and in servitude by various means, from laws and rules enforcing segregation through suppression of their right to vote to the frequent and open use of violence. Even in the north, black people were commonly understood to be less than whites. In the south, many blacks continued to farm as tenants and sharecroppers, landbound slaves without papers; while those who went north lived in poor conditions and generally worked as unskilled laborers. In the south, Jim Crow laws enforced racial segregation, but even in the north the slaves' descendants lived largely segregated from the white population.

If you have any doubt that slavery still was thriving in the United States a full hundred years after legal emancipation, please go to Appendix I right now and read the excerpts there from Letter from Birmingham Jail. In 1963 Martin Luther King, Jr., was a superbly educated young American with the brilliance to have done anything with his life. Just look at the way that man could write! But he was as much enslaved in America a hundred years after the Emancipation Proclamation as had been any of his slave ancestors. That white Americans have called the condition of their darker countrymen before 1965 anything other than a variant of slavery has been a parsing of words that has not served us well.

American Slavery Today

Slavery could have been ended with the signing of our Constitution in 1787. It could have been ended gently in the 1800s with a public education program focused on getting federal abolition laws passed, followed by sufficient education and support as each newly-freed slave began to live in full citizenship. Even as late as 1900, slavery could have been all over if the will to finish the job that legal emancipation had begun had not died with President Lincoln's assassination amid the malaise of a war-exhausted nation. But since emancipation never fully happened, the condition of abasement, economic bondage, and the risk of violence if they tried to rise was a bitter fact of American life for nearly everyone with darker skin right through the first half of the twentieth century.

Yet wonderfully, despite the long odds against them, by the nineteen-fifties many descendants of freed slaves were entering the American middle class. A million men who were melanin-enriched had served their country in the Second World War; and even though most of them were in segregated and service- based positions, just their participation in that war had begun to shift the boundary between races in the same way that women's working in American factories during wartime had begun to shift the boundary between genders. America's ideal of a post- racist and post-sexist country may not have been adopted for a few more decades, but it had its roots in the more equal nation that came out of the Second World War.

That more-equal-feeling America of the nineteen-fifties soon spurred a push to, for heaven's sake, desegregate the South a full hundred years after legal abolition. In the early sixties these efforts caused the festering boil that slavery still was to burst in the unpleasant ways that boils will burst. By the mid- nineteen-sixties it was clear that we had to do something! But as had been the case since the Civil War, it never occurred to anyone that slavery itself might still be the problem. We fixed that, right? Emancipation? How could slavery still matter? Sure, the tree of liberty is growing crooked, but things are getting better! At least that tree no longer bears the "strange fruit" of lynching victims.

Because it still didn't realize that slavery was America's fundamental disease, in the mid-sixties our federal government decided to throw money and social programs at some of modern slavery's most vexing symptoms. As a result, the black family in the United States was all but destroyed, and most of those green shoots of progress being made by the descendants of America's slaves that had been appearing since the Second World War soon withered.

What on earth could have happened?

President Johnson's Great Society is what happened. We may not have meant to pay poor mothers to evict the fathers from their children's lives, but for fifty years that has been the result. *And children need both parents!* Boys, especially, need their fathers. *If you want to understand the stubbornly high rate of black poverty today, and the appalling rate of black male incarceration, you need look no further than America's absurdly named "war on poverty" for an explanation.* And when you consider our alarming national debt, now approaching twenty trillion dollars, just be aware that our national debt has largely tracked our means-tested social programs. Our entire cataclysmic national debt today is trillions of dollars *less* than the $22 trillion that has been spent in the past fifty years to maintain a gentle kind of slavery and destroy the dreams of millions of American children.

As an aside, we should note that not all the recipients of fifty years of American welfare programs have been melanin- enriched. But while for white Americans welfare has offered a springboard out of poverty, for the descendants of slaves who never had been assimilated into American life it has been what amounts to a re-enslavement, this time by a benevolent federal government that gives them cars and wide-screen TVs while it makes no attempt to end their ongoing economic and social bondage.

Some have tried to explain the modern social problems of black Americans as cultural. They had no families during slavery times, so what do they know about families now? This notion is, to use a term politer than the one that we are tempted to use, pure hogwash. Even during centuries of slavery in America, those who were enslaved were forming families. They gave their children unique names so if the family ever were sold apart they would recognize those children later, and bonded couples who might have different owners remained faithful spouses throughout their lives. Perhaps family ties are even more important to people who have nothing else.

After legal emancipation, keeping families together became easier. During the hell of Reconstruction, the horror of Jim Crow, and every other kind of misery that was visited on America's melanin-enriched population during the century following 1865, they still kept their families proudly intact. *The census held in 1960 shows about the same percentage of intact black families as intact white families.*

But the nineteen-eighty census shows that in the intervening twenty years most of those black families had broken up.

We ask you to pause here and think about that. What centuries of legal slavery followed by a further century of debasement and outright brutality could not do to black American families was accomplished in less than two decades by a well-meaning but clueless federal government.

All of this has been tough to write. We know that it has been tough to read. But mincing words and papering things over and useless promises and halfway attempts have accomplished nothing in the past hundred and fifty years but the miserable impoverishment of millions of Americans, the splitting-apart of American society, the blighting of millions of black children's lives, and the alarming indebtedness of this nation that was supposed to be the world's best hope. Unless we can recognize failure and call it by its name, we are going to keep repeating the same mistakes. And the world has no more time for that now.

In the chapters to come we will analyze some of the symptoms and effects of modern slavery, and then we will talk about how we might at last cut away that foundational rock so it never will trouble this nation again.

Chapter Two
Understanding and Overcoming Bigotry

"I don't like that man. I must get to know him better."
— Abraham Lincoln,
16th president of the United States (1809–1865)

"I should like to know if, taking this old Declaration of Independence, which declares that all men are equal upon principle, you begin making exceptions to it, where will you stop? If one man says it does not mean a Negro, why not another say it does not mean some other man?"
— Abraham Lincoln,
16th president of the United States (1809–1865)

"I have a dream that my four little children will one day live in a nation where they will not be judged by the color of their skin, but by the content of their character."
— Martin Luther King, Jr.,
winner of the 1964 Nobel Peace Prize (1929–1968)

"America did not invent human rights. In a very real sense human rights invented America."
— Jimmy Carter, 39th president of the United States

"When even one American—who has done nothing wrong—is forced by fear to shut his mind and close his mouth—then all Americans are in peril."
— Harry Truman, 33rd president of the United States (1884–1972)

"Darkness cannot drive out darkness; only light can do that. Hate cannot drive out hate; only love can do that."
— Martin Luther King, Jr., winner of the 1964 Nobel Peace Prize (1929–1968)

We had meant this chapter to be a quick introduction to how we might best overcome bigotry in ourselves and in others. But we have found that even trying to define the word "bigot" is a minefield for those of us who are hoping to design a better future!

- Wikipedia defines "bigot" as "a prejudiced or closed-minded person, especially one who is intolerant or hostile towards different social groups (e.g. racial or religious groups), and especially one whose own beliefs are perceived as unreasonable or excessively narrow-minded, superstitious, or hypocritical."
- Merriam-Webster says that a bigot is someone who is "obstinately or intolerantly devoted to his or her own opinions and prejudices; especially one who regards or treats the members of a group (as a racial or ethnic group) with hatred and intolerance."

A primary problem with both definitions is that they are judgmental. If we hope to bind this nation's wounds from a war now a century and a half gone by, the last thing we want is to make people feel even more justified in judging others! Every American past the age of reason is a member of the walking wounded. It doesn't matter what your race or ethnicity might be; you, too, bear the scars of America's inability ever to get past slavery. For some, these scars take the form of strong opinions held about groups of people, often based on what our parents have taught us or based upon news items or unfortunate encounters. For others, these scars are feelings of guilt or shame about things that long predate our births; and for still others they are feelings of paranoia about saying anything about anything at all for fear of the pernicious thought-police.

These scars that each of us bears are a subtle but highly vexing symptom of the burden of slavery on modern America. And since we all have been harmed in this, we must be careful in defining the word "bigot" so we won't make anyone's damage still worse. With that in mind, here is a new definition of "bigot" that might help us usher in a better future:

A bigot is someone who has formed an opinion based upon incomplete information.

No judgment! Just understandable temporary befuddlement that might even be seen as endearing. That, plus an obligation on the part of the rest of us to gently help the sufferer with his or her learning.

Our goal is to bring all Americans together as a first step toward uniting the world. Your own goal may be different, but whatever it is, you can see that slavery has tied us all in knots. *Nothing worthwhile will ever again be accomplished in the United States until after we have removed that rock and properly replanted our tree of liberty.*

This means that we can no longer enjoy the luxury of shaming people for something so trivial as holding bigoted views! Instead, every American who may have negative feelings about other Americans of any shade must be gently helped toward a broader understanding. No matter what our nutty Uncle Albert says, or no matter what someone shouts at us on the street, it is our responsibility to respond as Martin Luther King, Jr. would want us to respond: with love, understanding, and a patient effort to gently help to educate the damaged and the lost.

Some Stereotypes Are Not Unfounded

If you get out into the world at all, you soon will see that to a surprising extent our racial and ethnic stereotypes will hold true. I know Italians who nurture epic grudges, Jewish people who are money-obsessed, light-hearted Hispanics, studious Asians, a passel of red-nosed Irish drinkers, and descendants of slavery who got rhythm. Naturally we begin to generalize, and that fact used to annoy me so much that I took out my frustrations on anyone who vexed me by fitting the stereotypes I was hoping not to see. I recall being irritated with a wonderful Irish friend for drinking; lecturing a client of Italian heritage about his need to get over his anger; and being so annoyed with a Jewish client who wanted me to squeeze someone on a deal that I lectured him about being the very reason why Jews have a bad reputation. *I was young then! I know better now, and I have learned to find pleasure in all these amusing ethnic and racial variations.*

Here is how you can do that, too:

- **Accept the fact that many group stereotypes are based on people's observations.** Well, they are! Whether these characteristics are genetic or cultural or a mixture of both, there are some details about people which often seem to be influenced by race, culture, or gender. And we can no longer afford the luxury of denouncing simple statements about observed facts as if they were the fruit of malicious bigotry.
- **Forgive people for being who and what they are.** Appendix III has a wonderful exercise in learning how to forgive everything so your entire life will stay forgiven! I urge you to use this little trick to get past

any stereotypical characteristics in others that might really bother you.

- **Learn to love all our racial, ethnic, and gender variations.** I've discovered that the reason I was trying to get people not to be the way they actually were was that I hated seeing them living up to (or down to) common stereotypes. And that was my problem. Once I forgave people for being themselves, I was able to begin to see their stereotypical eccentricities as actually adorable. So what if he drank a lot? Who cared about her craving for money? And one stereotypical characteristic of many descendants of slavery is a spiritual depth and wisdom that you will come to see as beautiful.

All the stereotypical characteristics of Americans are the zesty spice in our melting pot. They flavor life without getting in our way, and all of us would be poorer without them. So when you see people behaving in ways that seem to you to be predictable based upon race, ethnicity, or gender, learn to smile and see these characteristics as wonderful. When you see other people's behavior always as enriching and endearing, you move beyond bigotry and into the realm of appreciation and delight. We have nothing to fear—and much to enjoy—in accepting those around us as they really are.

America's Core Racial Bigotry

Although forming any opinion about another human being unless you know that person well is going to be counterproductive, there is one particular kind of bigotry now pervasive in American culture that forms some of modern American slavery's most vicious and intractable chains. Holding this particular bigoted view of black people actually is seen as a virtue! And tragically, it often is taught to children. Always with the best of intentions. ***Some call it "the soft bigotry of low expectations," but there is nothing soft about it.*** Simply put, this sort of bigoted view assumes that darker skin connotes a lessened ability to learn and to compete in life. Sometimes skin shade even is seen to excuse an unwillingness to work for a living, or an actual inability to tell right from wrong. It is this kind of bigotry that insists that no attempts be made to help those on welfare to better themselves, and that likewise requires that colleges must lower their standards and accept black students whose tested abilities are less than those of the white people who will be studying beside them. Oh, sometimes the explanation given for such bigotry is that schools have been inadequate or that racism has blighted someone's life, but always there is that implicit suggestion that this poor soul is in some way inferior.

This is bigotry, pure and simple! And there is nothing soft or kindly about it.

It is your authors' contention that low expectations are becoming the most common form of racial bigotry in America. For so long as most Americans feel that the poor dears can't survive without our help, we never will end slavery's hold on this country. Thirteen percent of Americans will forever be seen as something like our beloved Aunt Wilma, who never has been right in the head so we always will have to subsidize her rent.

The irony in this is that the twenty-first-century descendants of American slavery may be the group among us who are the fittest of all to really prosper! Consider:

- **Legal slavery and its botched aftermath effectively culled those who were unfit.** People not physically strong and mentally agile were unlikely to survive the Passage, and once here they could not have survived the ruthless weeding that slavery imposed. The period of Reconstruction and then Jim Crow meant that for the first century after Abolition they lived in a minefield where only the fittest of them were able to do well. If you were trying over centuries to breed a group of people to be healthy and clever survivors, it is hard to imagine a more effective method.
- **Success in school is among the least efficient measures of what it takes to succeed.** I have been an attorney for the owners of closely-held businesses for more than thirty years, and many of these very successful people have told me they were struggle-to-get-a-B sorts of students. A surprising number never bothered with college. We have a hunch that if you gave academic aptitude tests to ten thousand people from off the street, you would find that as a group most Asians might score a bit higher than the group's average, while most who are melanin-enriched might score a bit lower. Pardon us if we yawn. This means nothing.
- **Keeping a race of people as cultural pets is the height of immorality.** In America we long have worshipped some very successful black artists and athletes, but if you look closely you will see a certain creepiness to what we are doing. We don't see their abilities as probably only typical of their race as a whole, but

instead our adulation seems to be more like the sort of encouragement we would offer if someone had trained a bear to walk on its hind legs, combined with a self-congratulatory sense that if we admire this athlete or that singer, then we aren't really racists after all. If extraterrestrials arrived here today and looked at the way we Americans still treat the melanin-enriched among us, they would assume these people must be a class of sub-humans that we support as cultural pets and we enjoy watching the better-trained among them perform for us.

It is time to accept the fact that every form of bigotry we might be nurturing is a flaw in us that we must strive to overcome. And this includes even the current vogue for blaming white males for all the world's problems in order to take them down a peg and thereby hope to elevate others. Good grief, how can we ever unite people if we keep coming up with new ways to divide them? Whenever we see folks that we don't know well and draw any conclusions about them at all, we are erecting barriers against the possibility of our ever connecting with them as people. And by giving ourselves permission to hold such biases, we are contributing to the debasement of us all.

Eradicating Bigotry From America

Forming instant opinions about other people and grouping as foreign those who look different from ourselves might have been early human survival skills. So we can excuse ourselves for automatically having done it in the past; but if we hope to create a better future, we are going to have to shed these tendencies which are of no more use to us now, and which in fact are very harmful.

And we can do that. You will be surprised to see how easy it is to reprogram your mind not to draw even one more bigoted conclusion! Personally, I am encouraged to recall that when I was a child my white doctor was to me the spitting image of Nat King Cole. I didn't see skin color as important until the culture taught me that it was important, and as I have watched my preschool-aged grandchildren at play in mixed-race Texas I have noticed that they, too, don't seem to see color. I have a hopeful hunch that this is going to be true of all American children, once we stop teaching them otherwise.

If you have trouble getting past your own bigotry programming, you might try learning what Jesus in the Gospels refers to as "forgiveness." In fact, what he teaches is a simple method for retraining your mind not to let things bother you, and it works so easily and so well that once you learn to do it your whole life will improve. Check out Appendix III for more information.

For now, though, let us together imagine an alternative America that long ago vanquished slavery. Once we consider how that better America might look, it will be easier for us to spot and to address all of modern slavery's distortions.

Chapter Three
Imagining a Slavery-Free America

"Nothing is unchangeable but the inherent and unalienable rights of man."

—Thomas Jefferson,
3rd president of the United States (1743–1826)

"Four score and seven years ago our fathers brought forth on this continent, a new nation, conceived in Liberty, and dedicated to the proposition that all men are created equal."

—From the Gettysburg Address, Abraham Lincoln,
16th president of the United States (1809–1865)

"You have young men of color in many communities who are more likely to end up in jail or in the criminal justice system than they are in a good job or in college. And, you know, part of my job, that I can do, I think, without any potential conflicts, is to get at those root causes."

—Barack Obama, 44th president of the United States

"There is nothing wrong with America that faith, love of freedom, intelligence, and energy of her citizens cannot cure."

—Dwight Eisenhower,
34th president of the United States (1890–1969)

"If you have always believed that everyone should play by the same rules and be judged by the same standards, that would have gotten you labeled a radical 60 years ago, a liberal 30 years ago and a racist today."

—Thomas Sowell, American economist, political philosopher, and social theorist

"If physical death is the price that I must pay to free my white brothers and sisters from a permanent death of the spirit, then nothing can be more redemptive."

—Martin Luther King, Jr., winner of the 1964 Nobel Peace Prize (1929–1968)

It's time for us to try a thought-experiment. Let's imagine a different United States in which a wise and benevolent federal government begins in 1800 to educate its citizens about the evils of slavery. Within a generation a growing national aversion to the institution begins to feed an up-swelling clamor in most of the country to end it altogether. In 1860 we elect Abraham Lincoln to be our 16th President, and we also elect a passel of Congressmen and Senators who have run on a platform of abolition. In 1862 a bill is passed and signed that will end American slavery on the first day of January, 1870, following a multi-year program during which the federal government will purchase and then free and naturalize every slave.

There is much about this plan that is controversial. Many people are not convinced that blacks and whites can live together as equals; and of course there is the worry that these federal purchases will drive up the slaves' market values and make the whole project too costly. But President Lincoln appoints the great abolitionist Frederick Douglass as his Secretary of Freedom (a new Cabinet position), and Douglass aggressively recruits freed slaves and sends them on tours of receptive statehouses and churches so they can mingle and tout their various accomplishments. Abolitionists soon form groups in most northern cities that will take in the former slaves as they are freed and will house and teach and advocate for them.

True, at first the promise of a federal market for slaves does drive up their prices, but after 1865 the fact that the value of a slave will soon be zero causes prices to decline so rapidly that when in 1880 a first history of this period is written, the actual cost of purchasing and freeing every American slave, even including their initial living subsidies paid through 1875, is found to have been barely half of what the calculated value of those slaves was in 1860.

Because of all the groups set up in northern cities to assist them, the freed slaves are disbursed nationwide. About half of them remain in the south, but so many of them are in the north as guests and friends of people who are thrilled to help them that within a generation many children of former slaves are entering the middle class. They are teachers, tradesmen, shopkeepers, and clerks in many northern cities where they are so thinly scattered that making friends and working with colleagues across what soon are no longer racial lines is within a decade or two seen as normal.

The situation in the south is a little different. In the Deep South, as much as twenty percent of the 1870 population of each state consists of former slaves. There, Secretary Douglass early in the second Lincoln administration establishes a number of what are called Freedom Offices to assist the first generation of freed slaves. He has teams working with local police to keep order, and he places observers in southern statehouses to provide an early warning to his office if potentially unconstitutional laws are passed.

There are a few violent protests that cause the federal government to send troops into Louisiana, Mississippi, and Alabama, but great care is taken to be respectful of all American citizens and their property. A watchful federal judiciary makes certain that no impermissible state laws will stand, and the southern whites soon accept the fact that they have nothing much to gripe about. This federal abolition was fairly accomplished under the terms of their nation's Constitution. The freed slaves were purchased, and never was there a military threat by the north against the south. Under the watchful protection of a wise and benevolent federal government, within a generation the southern blacks, too, are beginning to enter the middle class. By 1900 American is dealing with the more pressing problem of poor Southern European immigrants, while the third-generation descendants of former slaves live confidently in a peaceful country in which every citizen has a fair chance to rise.

Comparing a True Emancipation With What We Have Today

If the scenario that we have envisioned had happened, we would be living now an entire century past complete emancipation. How would that differ from our present situation? The differences would be too many to list, but here are what we see as the big five:

- **The races would be living comfortably mixed.** For generations all of us would have lived and worked with people of other races, much as many Texans now live and work in mixed communities. Whites would be used to seeing successful and productive people who are melanin-blessed, and we would have one national culture, enriched but not at all divided by its diverse racial and ethnic mix.
- **The descendants of fully emancipated slaves would not make white Americans uncomfortable.** What horrifies me most is the realization that it is specifically dark Americans with African features who are marked out by white Americans as different. Some Indian immigrants have very dark skin, but few white Americans are bothered by them. People who have lately come from Africa and speak with an accent also

don't spark unease. But there is even in the twenty-first century that appalling mix of guilt and shame between white and black Americans that still makes people uncomfortable. This insight even makes us wonder whether Barack Obama could have been elected president of the United States if his father had been descended from American slaves.

- **We would be a much more prosperous nation.** It costs money to semi-free a whole class of people and then to keep many of them unproductive. Just imagine an America with no national debt in which everyone was empowered to work and succeed!

- **We would know how to refer to one another.** The guilt and shame of this ongoing tail of slavery has driven us to think that we might ease our pain if only we could come up with a good way to refer to the slavery-impaired among us. Obviously the N-word is out, and apparently "Negro" is now falling from favor. For awhile "Afro-American" was hot, but now that seems to be insufficiently polite so "African-American" is what is preferred. Please! Are we serious? Kelley's ancestors have been in what eventually became the United States for as much as four hundred years, while my grandparents arrived in the twentieth century. If Kelley is an African-American, then I must be a Danish-American. My children would be Danish-English-French-Americans. What kind of sense does any of this make? And using the terms "black" and "white" may be worse, since there are very few black-skinned people and the only white-skinned people are albinos. Not to mention the fact that these terms date back to the worst days of chattel slavery. So now we suggest using neutral, factual terms like "melanin-enriched" and "melanin-deficient." But what will be glorious will be the day when we can refer to one another as just Americans! The only Americans who are stuck with hyphens should be our first-generation immigrants.

- **We would not be afraid of one another.** All the guilt and shame of slavery that still festers in America today has created in Americans of every shade a bone-deep anger and distrust of one another that is as impermissible as was the anger of all the white southerners whose lives were wrecked by the Civil War. Since neither black nor white Americans can allow ourselves to feel this anger, it festers instead as a vast unease around people who don't share our racial identity. And if a white person walking down a street sees a group of young black men approaching, he will cross the street at once. Just in case.

These five points offer only a hint of the myriad ways in which the American tree of liberty has grown sadly crooked because we never have managed to end slavery. Beyond them are all the lesser ills that easily could have been avoided, together with all the damage caused by our government's counterproductive halfway measures. The related destruction of poor white families; the appalling blight of America's cities; the increasing fractures of American society along ethnic as well as racial lines; and the gradual withdrawal of our wealthy elite into enclaves so they won't have to deal with this mess: compared with our present damaged state, a healthy America that was long past slavery would be unrecognizable now.

And over it all is the tragic waste of the lives of so many beautiful, frustrated, melanin-enriched men who learned as children that they were going to be superfluous except perhaps as breeders, and whose struggles to find some meaning in life, some way out of the slavery-lite that our culture has decreed for them, have landed so many of them in prison. Indeed, even darker-skinned American males who manage to avoid incarceration are much more likely than pale Americans to lead brutal and debased lives. For example, more than half of America's homicide victims are slavery's descendants. Nearly all their killers also are black.

It didn't have to be this way! To give you some perspective, you ought to know that from Reconstruction right through the nineteen-fifties the largely segregated neighborhoods in which most black people lived were anchored by watchful husbands and fathers and were so safe that few people locked their doors. But very soon after the war on poverty deprived many young men of their fathers, there began this awful slide into barbarism. ***Sorry. Another tough chapter to read.*** But it is impossible ever to fix a problem unless we are willing to understand its cause and to call it by its name! Given how hard this has been to read, we feel the need to urge you again to see our terrible present situation as no one's particular fault. It is essential that all of us believe that every player in this tragedy has done his best. The last thing anyone wants to do is to make our divisions even worse!

This is especially true since the primary cause of America's racial problems should be so easily addressable. ***We are confident that American slavery, and even most of its worst effects, can***

largely be ended in one generation and at no net cost to anyone if only we can muster the will to do it. But before we begin to talk about solutions, I want you to meet my friend Kelley Glover and to hear her American story.

Chapter Four
A Stranger in a Strange Land

Kelley Glover

"I had crossed the line. I was free; but there was no one to welcome me to the land of freedom. I was a stranger in a strange land."
—Harriet Tubman, American abolitionist and Civil War hero (1822–1913)

"Experience demands that man is the only animal which devours his own kind, for I can apply no milder term to the general prey of the rich on the poor."
—Thomas Jefferson, 3rd president of the United States (1743–1826)

"It was that which gave promise that in due time the weights should be lifted from the shoulders of all men, and that all should have an equal chance. This is the sentiment embodied in that Declaration of Independence."
—Abraham Lincoln, 16th president of the United States (1809–1865)

"We thought I was going to be a great athlete, and we were wrong, and I thought I was going to be a great entertainer, and that wasn't it either. I'm going to be an American Citizen. First class."
—Dick Gregory, American civil rights activist, comedian, and entrepreneur

"I am a woman who came from the cotton fields of the South. From there I was promoted to the washtub. From there I was promoted to the cook kitchen. And from there I promoted myself into the business of manufacturing hair goods and preparations. . . . I have built my own factory on my own ground."
—Madam C.J. Walker, American entrepreneur, philanthropist, and activist (1867–1919)

R*oberta and I have been friends for years without much talking about race.* Then as we began to shape this book, she was more and more confounded by the things I said until eventually she insisted that I had to tell you what it really is like to be Black in America. I was surprised at first. How could you not know? But she insisted.

I'm one of the lucky ones. My father fought hard to get an education through the Ph.D. level, and despite his dark color the feeling of inferiority that affects most Black men in this country never seems to have gotten him down. As his daughter, I went to Howard University and then to the Eastman School of Music for a Master's Degree. I am as middle-class as any White American. So the fact that I still am stuck for life with having to obsess about my skin color should shock you! My life is very much like yours, but still I have to live with this?

It is 1975. I am six years old, and I'm so very eager to learn. I have always loved books. I knew how to read by the age of four, and I looked forward to reading books with my mom, dad, brothers, and sister every day. Reading aloud and having books read to me made me feel so alive, so smart, and so special! So you would think that trips to the library at my new elementary school would be exciting for me. But they were not. ***I was one of three Black children at West Mercer Elementary School in Mercer Island, Washington.*** As I said in my Introduction, I had already experienced being shunned by African Americans who were "color-struck" and viewed me as less than they were for being a dark-skinned little girl. But moving from Detroit, Michigan to a mostly White area was *not* made easier by my school's librarian. You see, our librarian would allow one student per week to sit in her special chair as she read us stories. It was so *exciting* to know that *one day* the time would come when I would *finally* get to sit in her special chair as she read to my first grade class! So when the day *finally* came for me to sit in that chair, she asked, "Okay! Who hasn't sat in my special chair yet?" I eagerly raised my hand and waited for her to call me up. I kept waving my hand because she seemed not to see me. Eventually, all eyes were on me. But instead of calling me up to sit in the magic place, she leaned in towards me, looked me in the eyes, and said, "Oh! No one! We'll start all over again!"

I was confused. I saw her looking at me. I then looked around to see if people could see me. I thought that somehow I had become invisible! Clearly I had my hand up, and clearly she saw me because she looked right at me when she said, "No one!" The whole class was staring at me, looking as confused as I was. Then I started to feel so small. So inadequate. I felt my *self* disappearing . . . . . . disappearing into nothingness, as if I were truly invisible and my presence was the presence of nothingness. I suddenly felt ashamed. I didn't know *why* I felt ashamed, but . . . I just did. And I felt even smaller still, and more ashamed and more invisible as she called up another child to sit in her chair. No one spoke up for me and said, "She has her hand raised!" "What about Kelley?" They were probably as confused and dumbfounded as I was.

That was the *first* time in my six years on this planet that I felt as if my presence did not matter. I felt unsafe, embarrassed, ashamed, confused, and invisible. Her message to me and to the entire class of White children was, "Kelley, you do not matter." "This little *black* girl does not matter." To this day, I wonder how many of those children in my class remember that as clearly as I do; and if so, how did it make *them* feel? (*YES! Racism affects everyone!*) It did not matter that she was looking into the eyes of a child who was later tested and placed in the gifted and talented program. All she saw was Black. To her, Black people did not matter.

I internalized that moment and carried it with me until my senior year of college. I had managed to go through four years at Howard University without setting foot into the library even *once!* (Mind you, we're talking the 1980's and early 90's now, so not going into the library was much harder to do because you couldn't look things up on the Internet as students do today.) But as a senior in college I finally was *forced* to go into the library after being hired to be a research assistant for one of my professors. I had to work in Howard's Moorland-Spingarn Research Center, and also at the Library of Congress! Can you imagine? *Me?* This young woman who had been shown over and over again by a racist school librarian that I was dumb and did not matter now had to do research in two world-renowned libraries?

And I was so afraid. I was afraid that the librarians would kick me out for being dumb; I really believed that. I felt like I didn't belong there. I wanted to tell my professor to find another research assistant because I felt like I didn't belong in a library. *I STILL BELIEVED THAT I WAS DUMB! I STILL BELIEVED I DID NOT REALLY MATTER!* I can only imagine how other children must feel who lack the advantage of a nurturing, two- parent, upper-middle-class home.

Which brings me to my parents, who instilled a strong sense of self in each of their four natural and four adopted children. My mother was a stay-at-home mom with a strong sense of spirituality about her, and she taught us that God lives inside of us and inside of every living creature so our true power lies within. She had been born in the rural south as a sharecropper's daughter, then later her family had moved to Michigan to find a better way of life. She was raised to believe that human beings were born into sin and were wretched souls who went to hell if they did not follow the ways of the Good Book, but she never believed in any of that! She taught us that God is only Love, and that the Love of God lives in each of us. *My father also was born into poverty as a sharecropper's son.* His family left the segregated South when he was a child, and they also ended up in Michigan. He grew up to earn a Ph.D. Then he became a community college president; the co-owner of the first Black bank in Miami, Florida; the owner of a strip mall; and the founding president of Miami Dade Community College's Homestead campus, which he built from its blueprints to the institution that it is today. All my blood siblings are college-educated. And when my parents were in their fifties, they kindly adopted four more children and tried to raise them with the same sense of self-worth that they had attempted to instill in us.

I say all of this to illustrate a point. Even with all that positive energy supporting me . . . still I felt myself to be less than others. And not just because of that school librarian, but because I had absorbed all the messages that Black people get from America's media and from the teachers and guidance counselors who discourage us from taking AP classes or applying to the best universities. I'm talking here about teachers and counselors who may not be blatant with their racism, but who expect Black young people and our families to be satisfied with doing just enough to get by.

However, I think that because of how I was raised, *eventually* I had enough insight to examine myself and ask, "Where are these irrational fears and feelings of deep inadequacy coming from?" That was when those first-grade memories of that librarian came flooding back. It really hurt. That one year of being called dumb and being told that I was no one had had a profound effect on me; and because I never told anyone in my family, I carried that burden all through elementary school, junior high, high school, and college. From that moment of realization on, I was *determined* to be the *best* damned researcher and writer that I could be. I was *not* going to allow her racist attitude to hold my mind and spirit in bondage anymore!

This feeling of being what I have come to call "the visible invisible" is what many Black people (and indigenous people, like Native Americans) feel every day. Why do you think "Black Lives Matter" resonates with so many people of color? When you receive the kind of treatment that I got from my old librarian, it does something to you on a cellular level. On a soul level. People of color from Asia, India, Africa, and Latin America all struggle within our *own* communities, fighting off shame that stems from centuries of having been enslaved and/or colonized or put onto reservations by Europeans. *Centuries* later, we still are playing out those roles of shame and guilt with each other. Shame for not looking white enough within communities of color. Or plagued by the White guilt that aware people of European descent feel for what their ancestors have done historically to people of color. And on the other end of the spectrum, there still is a belief in some Whites that they are genetically superior to non-Whites.

The stigma of being "too black" affects so many of us, although some will deny it. There are people who to this day *still* tell me that I am too dark to hang out in the sun! I was recently chastised by an older Black woman for sitting outside to warm up from the too-cold air conditioning inside her home. She came outside, saw that I was sitting on her lawn in the sun, and said,

"*What* are you doing out here, as Black as you are? You don't want to get any blacker, do you? Get outta that sun!" I still hear school-aged children say, "Well at least I'm not Black," or, "At least I'm not nappy like you." And these are fighting words, by the way. To be called Black (as in dark-skinned) or nappy (as in having tightly curled hair) is a huge insult in the Black community. Sad, but true.

Most recently, when I was backstage getting ready to tape a TV show, one of the young Black teenaged guests exclaimed before someone took a photo of us, "Oh no! I'm a *red*-bone! (Translation: I'm light-skinned.) It's too dark over here, and I am *not* dark-skinned. I need to show that I'm light! I'm a red-bone!" To which her twin sister replied, "As if something is wrong with being dark."

Colorism still swims around our consciousness like a flesh-eating parasite eating away at our brain cells. As the old saying in the Black community goes, "Light, you all right. Brown, stick around. Black, stay back!" And on the other end of the spectrum you hear very light-skinned White people being ashamed of having such pale skin. You have White people with light-colored skin who risk getting skin cancer to make their skin darker, or they apply bronzer, or they get spray-tans to look darker than they really are. Ironic, isn't it? To me, it's all madness. Why can't people of all backgrounds *celebrate* our various and beautiful skin tones, and not make one out to be better than another?

So, how do we get over our ego selves? How do we stop hearing that incessant voice that insists that we are not good enough, or that we are much better or more worthy than some other human beings? First, we have to become aware of our thoughts, both our own thoughts and our thoughts as a collective. As a person of color, it helps me that I now understand where colorism comes from, so if you also need to understand the source of colorism before you can get past it, I will explain. During slavery, the offspring of the slave master were called "house slaves." They were half white, half black, and usually they had lighter skin and straighter hair than the darker-skinned "field slaves." They were sometimes given their freedom, and often they received preferential treatment since they were the offspring of their White owners.

After Emancipation, some lighter-skinned blacks were light enough to "pass" and they assimilated completely into the White culture. Others formed "Blue Vein Societies" and institutions such as colleges, clubs, and churches that did not allow Black Americans who were darker than a brown paper bag (the paper bag test), or they had to show their blue veins in their lighter skin in order to be a part of that particular institution. Light-skinned blacks who were a part of the "black bourgeois" or "Blue Vein Society" had higher social standing, could mix and mingle with each other, could marry other light-skinned blacks and expected to have light-skinned children. (Now do you understand why my neighbors in Detroit did not want their son to play with me?) Today this attitude can still be seen, not just among American Blacks but also in Latino communities and in Asian communities. It is called colorism, or internalized racism, and is seen in all the parts of the world where European colonialism and the enslavement of people of color ever have occurred. These shackles of the mind still haunt many people of color today.

Another kind of enslavement is the self-enslavement of the mind that many African-Americans still live with unconsciously. For example, I did not realize until I went to another country that I was keeping my distance from merchandise for fear that a store owner might accuse me of stealing. It was 1996, and two of my fellow classmates at the Eastman School of Music and I attended a music conference in Paris, France. While there, I went into a small corner store to browse. I did as I always had done, and would pick something up only if I meant to buy it. As usual, I was telling myself, "Keep away. You know you're being watched. You do not want the police called on you—again—by a paranoid shop owner who thinks you've stolen something." And then I got the feeling that I wasn't being watched. And sure enough, I looked around and no one was nearby with a nervous eye on me. I was flabbergasted! *No one here looked at me and thought I was a criminal!!*

Can you imagine how freeing that felt? To be just a human being browsing and not having some negative label put on me? Having the liberating feeling of not having to try to make people feel more comfortable with me and not threatened by my shade of skin? Do you know how much brain cell energy it takes to always be monitoring yourself in that way? In that *instant*, I had the oddest feeling. For the first time as an adult, I felt completely human. My soul breathed one great sigh of relief. An enormous weight lifted off my shoulders. For just that moment, I no longer carried the burden of always carrying a "black = criminal" label! Later that evening, my Eastman classmates and I met up with another small group of African-Americans. We decided to catch a cab back to our hotel instead of riding the subway. We wanted to try something *radical!* We would have one of the Black men in our group hail a cab to see if the cab would actually stop. And guess what happened? The cab pulled over immediately and picked all of us up! It didn't pass us by just because a Black man was hailing the cab! We all celebrated. We all felt so *good!*

That was the moment when we realized four things that we later discussed over a meal:

This is what it feels like to be White in America.

1. *This* is what it feels like to be just a human being and not a "black" human. *Simply human!*
2. We vowed that we all would stop acting a certain way to try to make prejudiced people feel comfortable. We decided to go back to the U.S. and hold on to our humanity, no matter how people of other races perceived us.
3. And we understood how Africans in Paris must feel. *They* were the threat in Europe, just as we were the threat in the United States. People of African-American descent were seen as "Americans" in Paris, and not as a threat, because we did not live there. Why do you think so many African-American celebrities move to Europe? They have felt this wonderful, freeing feeling too!

So after leaving Paris, I concentrated on keeping that glorious feeling of just being human. I tried to become more aware of my thoughts. I wanted to "lose my mind and create a new one," as the wonderful author Joe Dispenza would put it! And I did. I did it because just being human felt so amazingly good that I wanted to hold on to that feeling—to hold on to my new awareness that there are no limits to my goodness, and that I am responsible for my happiness no matter what the circumstances may be. I deserve the best. I refuse to hold my spirit hostage to what I imagine that others think of me.

This is a powerful exercise for any human being. How other people perceive us is beyond our control! The only thing that *any* human being can control is our own thoughts, perceptions, and beliefs. Worrying about what others think and limiting your precious Self because you are aware of thoughts that others might have is what holds so many human beings back, and especially holds back people of color. What other people think of you is none of your business. Live your very best life, even when it looks and feels like hell around you!

So now I have turned myself into an American adult. I have left behind forever those days of having trash thrown at me and being called "nigger," or having a gun pulled on me by young white men in pickup trucks toting the Confederate flag, or having dirt kicked on me by my best friends who were White because they were trying to prove to their racist family members that, "See! We hate niggers too!" or being followed in a park by drunk White men who kept calling me and my parents niggers, or having the police called on me and my Black friends because the store owners thought we had stolen something, or teachers who called me dumb even though I was "talented and gifted." All of that is behind me now. I have had to let that and all other racist incidents that happened to me, to my family members, and to my friends, finally and forever GO! I value my own sanity, my own peace of mind. Holding on to other people's insanity will *make you* insane, bitter, and stuck. And I refuse to live like that!

Building Our Bright Shared Future

Chapter Five
Why Separations Among People are Destructive

"Whatever affects one directly, affects all indirectly. I can never be what I ought to be until you are what you ought to be. This is the interrelated structure of reality."
—Martin Luther King, Jr.,
winner of the 1964 Nobel Peace Prize (1929–1968)

"In the white community, the path to a more perfect union means acknowledging that what ails the African-American community does not just exist in the minds of black people; that the legacy of discrimination—and current incidents of discrimination, while less overt than in the past—are real and must be addressed."
—Barack Obama, 44th president of the United States

"I just want to do God's will. And he's allowed me to go to the mountain. And I've looked over, and I've seen the promised land! I may not get there with you, but I want you to know tonight that we as a people will get to the promised land."
—Martin Luther King, Jr.,
winner of the 1964 Nobel Peace Prize (1929–1968)

"I regard consciousness as fundamental. I regard matter as derivative from consciousness. We cannot get behind consciousness. Everything that we talk about, everything that we regard as existing, postulates consciousness."
—Max Planck,
German winner of the 1918 Nobel Prize in Physics
(1858–1947)

"'You shall love the Lord your God with all your heart, and with all your soul, and with all your mind.' This is the great and foremost commandment. The second is like it, 'You shall love your neighbor as yourself.' On these two commandments depend the whole Law and the Prophets."
—Jesus (MT 22:37–40)

"Love is the only force capable of transforming an enemy into a friend."
—Martin Luther King, Jr.,
winner of the 1964 Nobel Peace Prize (1929–1968)

If you know me at all, you know me as a small-business lawyer with a peculiar hobby. Two extraordinary experiences early in life have led me to spend the past fifty years studying centuries worth of abundant and consistent evidence of what actually is going on. My quest to understand reality began as an effort to figure out what had happened to me in childhood, and it led me through an amazing amount of afterlife evidence, quantum physics for dummies, the fruits of consciousness research, and even a fresh interpretation of the Gospel teachings of Jesus. By now I am one of a handful of people who study information from various sources in an effort to begin to comprehend the gigantic and complex totality of what reality must be. My studies have raised some big concerns about our pressing need to bring the whole world together, which of course cannot begin to happen until America has come together as a nation! So we have included this chapter about what seems to be true in order to help you better comprehend the stakes.

Reading it is optional. We think you might like to have this added perspective, but the rest of the book works fine without it so if you are either strongly atheistic or strongly religious, we ask that you read no further here but go right on to Chapter Six. We have no wish to interfere with your beliefs. But on the other hand, if you are open-minded and curious we invite you to join us for this brief detour.

The fresh conclusions about reality that we researchers are stumbling toward now could have been arrived at much more easily by mainstream scientists a century ago. But in the early part of the twentieth century the university departments and the peer-reviewed journals began to adopt materialism as what they then called "the fundamental scientific dogma." At the time they were grappling with the bombshell of quantum mechanics that just had exploded in their midst, and the last thing they were prepared to entertain was the flood of information then being received from people who were not in material bodies! Perhaps their brief withdrawal into materialism could have been excused a hundred years ago, but unfortunately university departments and peer-reviewed journals still largely enforce materialism to this day.

Of course, anything based in a dogma is essentially a religion, with all the need to enforce orthodoxy and to ignore contrary information that any faith-based system implies. Physicists have suspected or known for a century that even what seems to be solid matter is in fact just energy; but since that observation violates materialism, what should have been a gigantic insight has been more like an inconvenience. Rather than studying all the implications of the astounding fact that matter is energy, scientists have spent billions on mostly trying to understand how energy can express as solid matter. *Higgs boson, anyone?*

And this, despite the fact that Max Planck, the father of quantum mechanics, discovered a century ago that what we experience as consciousness is the base creative force. *He said in 1931, "I regard consciousness as fundamental. I regard matter as derivative from consciousness. We cannot get behind consciousness. Everything that we talk about, everything that we regard as existing, postulates consciousness."* He followed up this insight a little more than a decade later by saying, *"There is no matter as such. All matter originates and exists only by virtue of a force which brings the particle of an atom to vibration and holds this most minute solar system of the atom together. We must assume behind this force the existence of a conscious and intelligent mind. This mind is the matrix of all matter."*

Eureka! Max Planck had discovered God as scientific fact. By now, Dr. Planck's gigantic insight has been used to illuminate what reality researchers have been learning from those that we used to think were dead, and to build a first view of a complex reality that is more interesting—and much happier— than all of humankind's fondest imaginings. A separate book could be written about all that reality researchers have learned so far; but for our purposes, just the insight that our minds are part of the eternal Mind which continuously manifests this universe is enough for us to begin to grasp a simplified view of what is going on. Here are a few points that can help you appreciate what is at stake in our efforts to bring this nation together so we can unite the world:

- **The only thing that objectively exists is what we experience as human consciousness.** To paraphrase our friend Dr. Planck, consciousness has to pre-exist the universe because consciousness is where matter comes from.
- **Each of our minds is part of the Mind that continuously manifests the universe.** There are many implications of this fact, but perhaps the most profound is the simple truth that we all together are one being! Your brother really is yourself, which is something Jesus told us long ago.
- **Emotion governs the base creative consciousness.** Far from being just an artifact of minds that somehow arise from material brains, what we experience as emotion is the activating force of the only power there is. And consciousness expresses in a range of energy vibratory rates, from lowest (which is fear and other negative

emotions) to highest (which is consciousness's affinity for itself—or, to use a human term, perfect love).

- **Our minds are powerfully creative.** Since we all are part of that core creative energy, our thoughts are amazingly powerful. Few of us have any sense of that fact, so we have been recklessly harming one another and our planet just by thinking less lovingly and more fearfully.
- **Feelings of fear, hatred, anger, or even crankiness cause separations between us in the same way that physical combat would.** So for any of us to nurture bigoted thoughts is damaging to this country and to the world. For many of us to do it, even if we never express those thoughts, could play havoc with and destroy any hopes that we might have of ever bringing people together.

We understand how weird all of this may sound at first! But it is our negative feelings about others that we have to fight, and not just the physical or verbal expressions of them. In a truly healthy United States, everyone would be so well informed and so comfortable with everyone else that bigotry would be just an oddity of history. Then at last our better future could begin!

The fear-based thoughts that bigotry produces are contributing to the debasement of this planet. They aren't the only problem, of course, since all negative thoughts serve to lower the consciousness vibration of all of humankind; but no one in the United States who lives anywhere but under a rock can avoid seeing bigotry against our fellow Americans as our most vexing problem. And the result of all this negative thinking has been the depression of the vibratory rate of consciousness energy over all the earth, to the point where we are entering what elevated beings tell us is a downward spiral that might well lead within two hundred years to the breakdown of civilization. Those that we used to think were dead are telling us how to reverse this process so we can instead create a beautiful future of abundance and unity for all of humankind. And they are telling us that the replanting of the tree of American liberty without that handicapping rock has got to be the first step! After a hundred and fifty years of trying to make slavery go away on its own by ignoring it and throwing money at it and claiming that just avoiding certain words can make it go away, it is time for us to put ending slavery directly front and center in America.

Whatever doing it right is going to cost is going to be cheaper than the alternative!

Of course, finally ending American slavery will be essential if we are ever to make free and happy lives possible for all of slavery's descendants. Even if that were the only reason to do it, surely it would be enough! But it also turns out that ending slavery and every one of its modern effects is going to be essential if we are ever to create a livable future for all of humankind.

Chapter Six
Why Some Possible Remedies Never Will Work

"These Negroes, they're getting pretty uppity these days and that's a problem for us since they've got something now they never had before, the political pull to back up their uppityness. Now we've got to do something about this, we've got to give them a little something, just enough to quiet them down, not enough to make a difference. For if we don't move at all, then their allies will line up against us and there'll be no way of stopping them, we'll lose the filibuster and there'll be no way of putting a brake on all sorts of wild legislation. It'll be Reconstruction all over again."

—Lyndon Johnson, 36th president of the United States
(1908–1973)

"There are no adequate substitutes for father, mother, and children bound together in a loving commitment to nurture and protect. No government, no matter how well-intentioned, can take the place of the family in the scheme of things."

—Gerald Ford, 38th president of the United States
(1913–2006)

"They might have wanted fathers and they might have wanted husbands. We have given them instead checks and a dole."

—Robert F. Kennedy, American Senator (1925–1968)

"It's heartbreaking to see so many people trapped in a web of enforced idleness, deep debt, and gnawing self-doubt."

—Bill Clinton, 42nd president of the United States

"Let us not seek the Republican answer or the Democratic answer, but the right answer. Let us not seek to fix the blame for the past. Let us accept our own responsibility for the future."

—John F. Kennedy, 35th president of the United States
(1917–1963)

It would be wonderful if just our good intentions were able to affect the results of our actions! If intentions mattered, every one of us would soon be a beautiful and admired billionaire. But unfortunately, there are some basic laws of human and financial physics that take over once a diet is undertaken or an investment is made or a bill is passed, and those immutable laws are what govern our results.

We must never doubt the fact that everyone over the past century and a half who has thrown ideas and money at slavery's symptoms has been trying to fix our problems! But nothing they have done has touched the fact of our botched emancipation hastily begun in the course of a disastrous civil war. And each of our ineffective attempts to address the results of that mistake has led to unforeseen consequences that have further stunted and twisted the tree of liberty on which so much now depends. *But we have some things that our ancestors did not have.*

At last we think we understand what has been causing all the problems they were unable to solve; and we also have the benefit of seeing the negative results of some of the attempts made to fix those problems. We have run out of time and money and run out of excuses, so this time we had better get it right! And we can do that. So long as we are willing to look at the whole situation without emotion and without indulging in useless finger-pointing, we can at last complete the emancipation of America's slaves and create a bright and hopeful new beginning for this nation, and then for the world.

Albert Einstein is quoted as having said, **"The definition of insanity is doing the same thing over and over again, but expecting different results."** Reportedly he also said, **"If you always do what you've always done, you'll always get what you**

always got." We must let that sage's wisdom be our guide! In any further attempts we make to address America's problems, we must avoid repeating past mistakes.

The conclusions that you will begin to draw as you think about aspects of this situation are going to be your own, but to start you off we will list for you the five big conclusions that we have drawn:

- **The only way to help people is to personally empower them.** Empowering those who had been held in bondage so they could begin to live as free people would have been the essence of the neglected completion of their long- ago emancipation; and the fact that all of our subsequent efforts to help have resulted in their descendants' disempowerment is a fundamental reason why they have failed. In whatever we might do now, the personal empowerment of each of the descendants of those slaves must be a central guiding principle.
- **Human dignity and self-worth must be protected and enhanced.** We have learned by now how fragile and how essential is human dignity! Why has it taken us so long to arrive at the common-sense understanding that the disadvantaged people we are trying to help still are people, after all?
- **Intact families are essential to a healthy society.** Here is something else that we should have known, but we have had to learn it again the hard way. Your authors both enjoy long- term marriages, as did our parents before us. We can testify that while no spouse is perfect, our lives and our ability to be productive have been

much enhanced by our being married. And having children and elderly parents to care for is a beautiful gift! For Americans to be encouraged to live in families is the best way to build a stable and prosperous nation.

- **Children need both parents.** Once we would have said that boys need their fathers, but there is evidence now that girls need fathers, too. For fifty years the United States has been conducting an experiment in rearing children in enforced single-parent homes, and much of what is wrong with America now is the result of the failure of that experiment. So it isn't only for the children's sakes that we must give them back their fathers! Restoring the central role of American fathers in their children's lives is going to be essential if we are ever to repair this nation.

- **Our efforts to help those blighted by slavery must bring all Americans closer together.** Another experiment that America has been conducting has been in trying to enhance the tribal feeling of the melanin-enriched among us as a way to make them feel better about themselves. Militant movements like Black Panthers and Black Lives Matter, and even more mainstream organizations like NAACP and The Urban League, all are examples of this idea. But of course, every effort made to carve thirteen percent of Americans even farther away from the rest of society not only has failed to make them feel better, but it also has tended to make the effects of modern slavery still worse.

There are other conclusions to be drawn, but these seem to us to be the big five.

It is clear that something major must be done, and soon. Surveys show that even after a century and a half of well-meant efforts to heal this nation, and even after the eight-year administration of a melanin-enriched president during which time social spending caused our national debt almost to double, many people feel that the gulf between the descendants of slavery and the rest of this nation actually is widening. It is our contention that the "something major" to be done must be a carefully planned completion of the emancipation of America's slaves that is based in love and has the enthusiastic support of most of the American people. We believe that doing anything less will continue to produce more disastrous results. But we also think that doing the right thing still is possible, and that it will work.

Chapter Seven
Proposing Thomas Jefferson's Solution

"Educate and inform the whole mass of the people . . . They are the only sure reliance for the preservation of our liberty."
—Thomas Jefferson, 3rd president of the United States
(1743–1826)

"Until justice is blind to color, until education is unaware of race, until opportunity is unconcerned with the color of men's skins, emancipation will be a proclamation but not a fact."
—Lyndon Johnson, 36th president of the United States
(1908–1973)

"You can choose a future where more Americans have the chance to gain the skills they need to compete, no matter how old they are or how much money they have. Education was the gateway to opportunity for me. It was the gateway for Michelle. And now more than ever, it is the gateway to a middle-class life."
—Barack Obama, 44th president of the United States

"It is easier to build strong children than to repair broken men."
—Frederick Douglass, American abolitionist, suffragist, and statesman (1818–1895)

"I never learned hate at home, or shame. I had to go to school for that."
—Dick Gregory, American civil rights activist, comedian, and entrepreneur

"A child miseducated is a child lost."
—John F. Kennedy, 35th president of the United States
(1917–1963)

Let's try another thought-experiment. What if in 1961 President John F. Kennedy and his brother, Bobby, had better understood what was causing all their country's current racial strife?

Bobby says to Jack one morning over a sunlit breakfast in the White House family quarters, "You know, these troubles really go all the way back to the Civil War." He sips his coffee.

Jack says, "Of course they do. It's racism. Human nature." He butters his toast.

Bobby says, "Maybe not. I think they just botched Reconstruction. Why don't we try fixing that? Finish the emancipation that Lincoln started?"

Jack says, "Sure. Give it a try. Sounds a lot better than beating people's heads together forever."

So they soon announce that careful study has shown that America's racial problems stem from the fact that the war that began a hundred years ago almost to the day simply didn't finish the emancipation process. They begin a nationwide campaign rooted in the public school system and bolstered by editorialists and PBS specials to help Americans better comprehend how destructive the Civil War really was, and how impossible it would have been at the time to complete the process of emancipating the slaves.

It is only background noise at first. But gradually more and more Americans who are being driven to frustration and despair by all the ongoing racial chaos kind of stroke their chins and start to say, "Hmmm. What if . . . ?"

Then in November of 1963 President Kennedy is assassinated. In his grief, Bobby becomes determined to make finally ending slavery his brother's core legacy, and he helps to shepherd a pair of bills through Congress. The Civil Rights Act of 1964 passes and is signed in July, and the Full Emancipation Act of 1964 becomes law in December. That second law is a harder sell. It is going to be expensive, but eventually it barely passes Congress when leading economists at Princeton and Yale release a joint study showing that the government will gain in additional tax revenues over the next fifty years more than twice what the law will cost to implement.

The Full Emancipation Act of 1964 is simple. Under its terms, every person born in America from 1960 through 1990 who has one ancestor who ever was held in slavery in the United States will receive the best private education federal money can buy, from kindergarten through graduate school. And that's it. When President Johnson tries to follow this law with his plan for a great society, there is no stomach for any more social spending. ***Let's finish emancipation first and see what happens.***

One early problem is the fact that few children have anything but family legends plus complexion to offer by way of establishing eligibility, so the new Freedom Department has to grant a lot of provisional certificates while it waits for government contractors to establish a public genealogy program. Meanwhile, entrepreneurs soon see a market. Within three years it is estimated that close to half of all American citizens with ancestors dating to the Civil War period have paid to have their ancestry traced.

A surprising number of melanin-deficient people turn out also to have a slave ancestor, and the projected cost of the Full Emancipation Act balloons. There are a few buyers'-remorse editorials when even some wealthy American children begin turning up at tony preschools with eligibility certificates in hand. But while racial issues are subsiding, the Vietnam War is heating up, so by 1968, when Jack's brother Bobby is assassinated in his turn, the Full Emancipation Act has more or less melded in people's minds with the Civil Rights Act. For most Americans, life goes on as before.

But the melanin-blessed community is electrified. In black churches and community halls, north and south, these children born in 1960 and later are the golden ones, the shining future, the reasons why fathers take extra jobs and mothers stay up late to double-check homework and to pack extra-special school lunches. A few commentators note that America's black population is behaving pretty much as their own immigrant ancestors had acted upon arrival, in sacrificing everything for the children who will do much better than their parents have done. Soon there is a baby boom of sorts, as young black couples are urged to marry early and to have more children.

Now let's travel forward a bit in time and shift our point of view.

It is 1984. You are walking down a street on the south side of Chicago, and there coming toward you is a group of young black men. Do you feel the need to cross the street? Of course not. You think, "college students," and maybe nod as they pass. **Now it is 1994.** You live in a trendy suburban neighborhood.

The house next door has gone on the market, and you notice that the realtor is arriving now to show it to a young black family. Do you worry that these folks might actually buy? Don't be silly. Your first thought is, "I hope they're doctors or MBAs this time, and not more of those gabby professor types."

And now it is 2008. The oldest Full Emancipation Act scholars are approaching the age of fifty, while the youngest are just entering college. Nostalgic stories are appearing in newspapers and on the Internet about these youngest students, some of whom are the children of couples who also both received federal scholarships. When these bright and confident young people are interviewed, they sometimes share their grandparents' tales of the terrible 1960s, when people still thought that skin color mattered. You read their stories, and even if you are old enough to remember those times you have trouble now recalling what all the fuss was about. The races have been living easily mixed in neighborhoods and workplaces and churches for decades, and that seems only normal after half a century during which these educated and empowered young people have been integrating naturally into the middle class. To the vast betterment of the lives of every American and every citizen of the world, this country's darker thirteen percent have become entirely unremarkable.

What is most notable to your authors as we experiment with this idea is realizing what never has happened. No families were broken up in the sixties and seventies, so there are many more intact American families of all shades. No gigantic national debt has been wasted on the perpetuation of a separate underclass, and in fact this country has been debt-free for decades. Most wonderfully of all, there have by now been two generations of melanin-enriched doctors and scientists and businesspeople and scholars, all working hard and paying taxes and doing much more for their country than their country ever has done for them.

Thomas Jefferson's Emancipation Plan

We are not the first people to dream this dream. In his youth, Thomas Jefferson was an ardent abolitionist. He may have felt that way from childhood, but his hatred of slavery seems to have been intensified by the counsel of his cherished wife, a woman whose inherited slaves included her half-white surrogate mother and her six mixed-race siblings. Jefferson's marriage spanned the Revolution, and much of what he wrote during that period— including the first draft of the Declaration of Independence— has you envisioning his ardent abolitionist wife coaching him and looking over his shoulder. He hated slavery, but he was a thoughtful realist so he understood that simply abolishing it legally and doing nothing more would be a recipe for disaster. He seems to have foreseen in surprising detail our ongoing mess since the Civil War.

Jefferson decided during the course of the American Revolution that he wasn't happy in public life, and in 1781 he retired to his family, his farm, and his books, as he cheerfully put it at the time. He had already led Virginia to become the first place on earth to ban the importation of slaves, and he was in the process of attempting to persuade his state toward a complete emancipation that he was then thinking through in some detail. He saw education as emancipation's centerpiece. He would have begun with the youngest generation, educated them well before he freed them, and given them a state of their own in the continent's interior so they could govern themselves and learn to prosper and eventually black and white could come together as equals, as would have happened in the course of time if slavery never had existed. This was the plan that he was forming when Martha died at the age of 33. And her death upended his life.

That Thomas Jefferson became a young widower after what he referred to forty years later as "ten years of unchequered happiness" seems to have broken him. Quite literally, he never was the same man afterward. Months later he went to Paris as an envoy, and it was then that he began the public life that led him eventually to become the 3rd President of the United States. America gained a founding statesman, and he was zealous about his work, but for him it seems to have been a consolation life.

Thinking About What We Might Do Now

Deeply understanding any problem is half of finding its solution. President Trump has promised big help for the melanin-enriched among us, so we are hopeful that he will listen open-mindedly to all our best ideas!

Alas, that easy solution of fifty years ago would be complicated now by the fact that half a century of running in the wrong direction has unnecessarily hardened racial antipathies and has created new social and financial problems. Still, we are confident that American slavery can be ended in the span of just a few decades if we will educate and altogether empower every member of a whole generation of American slavery's youngest descendants. What we'll be doing is cutting slavery's tail by creating thirty years worth of births in which everyone descended from slavery will become a well-educated potential achiever. No exceptions. We will have to empower them all!

Until now, the majority of Americans have with reason looked at their darker-skinned countrymen and assumed that they were probably less: less well reared, less well educated, less wealthy, and less successful. But soon, we all will be looking at our youngest countrymen with darker skins and rationally assuming that every one of them has been tenderly reared, supremely educated, and fitted to be a great success in life. Once we have made this universal three-decades cut across the whole of slavery's tail, this empowerment of slavery's descendants will have become America's new normal. From the beginning, empowerment will be normal for these children who never have known a lesser life; and soon it will begin to herald a hopeful new-normal future for us all.

Here is what your authors suggest that we do today:

- **Level With the American People.** Tell them, even at this late date, that the rampant destruction of the Civil War made a true emancipation at the time impossible, and since every other attempt to solve our racial problems has only made them worse, we are going to do now what should have been done a hundred and fifty years ago, and complete the emancipation of America's slaves so we can properly embrace their descendants.

- **Pass and Sign the Martin Luther King, Jr. Full Emancipation Act of 2018.** The name seems fitting for a number of reasons, including the fact that 2018 will mark the fiftieth anniversary of Dr. King's assassination. Under this Act, every American child born between 2010 and 2040 who has one ancestor ever held in slavery in the United States gets the best private education our money can buy, from kindergarten through graduate school. We think this is an historic moment when passing such a bill should be easy! President Trump has promised a new beginning for black children, and he has been blessed with a same-party Congress. Since the first Republicans began the emancipation process under President Lincoln, it is fitting that Republicans now will complete it. Although, as we think about it, why would any Democrat vote against this bill? If President Trump is as smooth and forceful about getting the backing of leaders of all shades as he has been in his business dealings, it is hard to imagine that such a bill would not pass Congress by acclamation.

- **Proclaim 2019 to be the Year of Jubilee.** As we look at the many ways in which the experience of American slaves and their descendants has differed from the experience of most Americans, we wonder if it matters that for them there never was an event of hopeful immigrant arrival, nor was there ever a proud and triumphal moment of citizenship naturalization. Instead, the descendants of American slaves have been treated as something like barnacles on our ship of state. We always have had to deal with them, but unlike most of their fellow Americans, those with ancestors who once were imported as slaves cannot look back and find the moment when those ancestors were welcomed as full Americans. (This is true of Native Americans, too, so perhaps they ought to share in this Jubilee.) Let's give the descendants of American slavery their symbolic Ellis Island and their symbolic open-arms welcome into the full citizenship that is their own! We can honor them all by celebrating all these beautiful African-American children for whom the best education and full participation in the American dream is now their birthright. Some sources date slavery in America to the arrival of the first African in Jamestown in the year 1619. It seems to us that four hundred years of second-rate status for melanin-enriched Americans is long enough, and also it seems that paler Americans will never stop feeling bad about slavery until they have shared in celebrating with their darker brethren an official end to it.

- **Integrate the Full Emancipation Act With State Educational Voucher Programs.** We already give every American child a publicly funded education through high school. If the federal government works closely with the states, it should be able to use what the states are now paying for these children's educations to fund some of the costs of their Full Emancipation tuitions to the best private schools.
- **Work Out Deals With Colleges and Universities.** We have proven by now that the best way to balloon the cost of anything is to throw government money at it. But a savvy Trump Administration can ensure that every college that gets Full Emancipation Act funds is teaching these children what they will need to learn in order to succeed in life while not wasting money in the process.
- **Offer Job Training to Older Descendants of American Slaves.** Experiments done under President Clinton to impose work requirements on welfare recipients were deemed to be largely successful in getting healthy people off the dole, but we think that President Trump can do better. Once their children are getting the best educations, many of the parents also are likely to want to improve their own lives. A program of government-paid vocational college and occupational training for all descendants of slavery who earn decent grades seems to us to be a great idea.

- **Maintain the Current Welfare System For Those Who Need It.** The only objection that we can imagine to the Full Emancipation Act of 2018 might be a worry that we would take care of the children but let their grandparents starve. We cannot do that. As a nation, we were the ones who set up those demeaning welfare rules, and people who have played by our rules have a right to continue to rely on our support. We tend to think that few people who are younger now than about age thirty are going to need it.

We hope that some American foundations will join in the effort to help this country at last live up to its best ideals. With federal resources more limited now, even the fact that Full Emancipation Act scholars are likely to return over time more in taxes and increased productivity than the government will have spent on their educations shouldn't make us feel that we can spend money wildly! So what would be wonderful would be if foundations and people with deep pockets would join in supplementing this great work. Perhaps they might make it possible for us to extend tuition help to some older students, to provide job training and small-business seed-money for the parents, to experiment with social enrichment programs.

Joining us all in this effort to complete emancipation would let the foundations help to fund a cause that ticks off so many of their goals! Help the poor? *Check.* End racism? *Check.* Make this country healthier and more prosperous? *Check and double-check!* **One role for America's most successful might be to counsel and support the parents of Full Emancipation Act scholars as some of those parents enter the world of business.** The best way to fight our urban blight will be to start to fill those empty storefronts! Incubators in each major city could teach basic business skills, and could act as unofficial partners and offer their counsel as new businesspeople try their wings. America's wealthy citizens in their country clubs might form mentoring programs for fledgling business owners. Venture capital firms could offer seed money and loans for slavery's descendants who have no established credit, perhaps with the assistance of favorable tax treatment; and even suburban families might help by coming into the cities on weekends to paint and plant trees and rehabilitate ravaged neighborhoods. The more Americans there are who take a personal stake in these efforts to help the melanin-enriched among us, the easier it will be to put every bit of the awful legacy of slavery behind us.

Two characteristics of what we have suggested seem to us to be crucial to any good plan:

- **We are making of the final ending of slavery a triumphal national set of events.** This is what Americans never have had, this moment when all of us together can celebrate the end of slavery and can welcome the descendants of slavery as the treasured fellow citizens that they are. White Americans need this cathartic moment of putting the past behind us as badly as do black Americans.
- **It will cost us little or nothing to implement.** By definitively turning each member of the next generation of slavery's descendants into a well-educated and fully empowered American citizen, we are making tax-paying producers out of millions who

would otherwise have been likely takers. We are ensuring that their children and grandchildren will be educated members of the middle class, and we are depriving America's prisons of forty percent of their likely future inmates. As we think about it, the economic return on this investment in what is now America's least productive class should give us back many times its cost!

Of course, whatever we consider doing must be governed by the five core lessons that were summarized in the previous chapter. After all, we learned those lessons the hard way. We must make sure to deeply understand our past now, since we cannot afford more mistakes!

Chapter Eight
Attacking Other Forms of Bigotry

"I believe that every human mind feels pleasure in doing good to another."

—Thomas Jefferson, 3rd president of the United States
(1743–1826)

"I know in my heart that man is good. That what is right will always eventually triumph. And there's purpose and worth to each and every life."

—Ronald Reagan, 40th president of the United States
(1911–2004)

"There is not a liberal America and a conservative America—there is the United States of America. There is not a black America and a white America and Latino America and Asian America—there's the United States of America."

—Barack Obama, 44th president of the United States

"I like the idea of amending the 1964 Civil Rights Act to include a ban of discrimination based on sexual orientation. It would be simple. It would be straightforward."

—Donald Trump, 45th president of the United States

"To sit back hoping that someday, some way, someone will make things right is to go on feeding the crocodile, hoping he will eat you last—but eat you he will."

—Ronald Reagan, 40th president of the United States
(1911–2004)

"It is in our lives and not our words that our religion must be read."

—Thomas Jefferson, 3rd president of the United States
(1743–1826)

T*his is the only chapter in this book that I passed to Kelley and had her read its first draft and say, "Girl, what are you thinkin'?"* She insists to me that racism and colorism still affect many more people in America than I ever had imagined, so I have modified the categories that follow. In particular, I have removed my pronouncement that discrimination against Asians and against Indian immigrants happily is a thing of the past, and I have added a plea that we remember that Native Americans are treated as subhuman to this day. It is Kelley's wish that our educational program to create a generation of superior and empowered black American citizens will be extended as well to Native Americans, and I bow to her wisdom. Now I echo her wish.

Still, we both believe that once this country has begun the process of completing the abolition of slavery, other forms of bigotry will lessen as well. That singular vast and complex problem has for generations so preoccupied us that it has hardened our hearts against others who also seem to be a bit different from what we envision to be the American mainstream. Let's look at some of these groups of people who also have been victims of American bigotry (which, we remind you, is the forming of opinions about others based upon incomplete information):

- **Asian Immigrants.** A century and more ago, immigrants from China, Japan, and India often were victims of the rankest persecution, but nowadays most new Asian immigrants are educated, they speak English, and they are familiar with American life. It has been our observation that Americans in general see Asian newcomers as a plus, but still they are affected to some extent by the ignorance that makes everyone whose appearance differs from the standard-issue pallid American seem to some to be perhaps a bit less.

- **Spanish-Speaking Americans.** One of the blessings of living in Texas is the fact that a third of the population here is Hispanic. Even though some speak little English, we have found new immigrants from south of the border to be especially hard-working and family-centered people. When I have on occasion talked with Hispanics about how well they have integrated themselves, I have learned that many of them are eager to have America close its borders. One said to me, "This is crazy! We're letting in the criminals!" Seeing how well most second- generation Hispanics have integrated in the state of Texas, our suggestion is that we close our border in order to protect every American, and that we also put out a million new visas a year for Mexicans, Cubans, and those from farther south. This way, we can keep up a healthy influx of wonderful future American citizens while we screen every immigrant who enters this country.

Why anyone would be opposed to this solution is something that we cannot imagine.

- **Native Americans.** Kelley and I have disagreed about whether we should include the appalling treatment of Native Americans as another of America's core sins. To me, the terrible confinement of these people on reservations to this day is a different problem, and I haven't wanted to blunt our message by addressing in this book any plight but that of Americans who are descended from African slaves. It is clear to both of us, though, that Native Americans suffer from the same government-enforced disempowerment and lives of meaningless debasement that has been foisted on the melanin-enriched among us, and we agree that further study would suggest that the same solutions that will work for black people will work for Native Americans as well.

- **Jews.** We cannot fathom why anyone would hold bigoted views against a group of people who have been productive Americans since our nation's founding, but we realize that the core Semitic stereotype may on occasion be rooted in experience. We urge you now to consider the fact that the special Jewish talent with money— if indeed that talent exists—may actually be a gift to us all! Consider the heroism of one Haym Salomon, without whose talents you might well be saluting a Union Jack today. Salomon came to North America in 1772, four years before our Revolution began, and he became a member of the Sons of Liberty and devoted himself to the cause of freedom. He was nearly hanged, but he never wavered in his daily efforts to raise the funds that our ragged army must have to survive. After the war, he repeatedly risked his business interests and frequently lent his own funds as he helped the colonies to forge a union powerful enough to stand on its own, and in the end he died a pauper. He had spent everything his business talents had earned him so you and I could be free today. Whenever you suffer a little bigoted thought about the

Jewish people around you, remember Haym Salomon and the millions of other Jews who have contributed so much to this nation's life.

- **The LGBTQ Population.** If American adults are free at all, we are free to choose to love anyone who also chooses to love us. If we aren't happy with something about our bodies, and if we have the funds to pay for alterations, then by all means we have the right to change our genders as surely as we have the right to change our faces. The most generous estimate that we have seen makes LGBTQ people just four percent of the population anyway, and they aren't out there recruiting so they pose no particular threat to you. That there is any bigotry against such people who simply think a little differently seems to be due almost exclusively to the dictates of one particular religion. Of course, Americans have the right to freedom of religion and freedom of association. What we don't have, though, is the right to ask the government to enforce our particular bigotries, and nor do we have the right to create further needless divisions among people. If you have negative feelings about LGBTQ people that are rooted in Christian teachings, please go to Appendix IV for a different view of how Jesus might prefer that you think.
- **Females.** I grew up in the nineteen-fifties, survived the sixties, and in the seventies attended law school at a time when only twenty percent of my class was female. If anyone should be a feminist, surely I should be that feminist! But I can now frankly say that I have always

found my gender to be an advantage, both in business and in life. With all our legal protections now in place, there is no more need for feminism as a cause in America than there is a need for masculinism. Of course, if you yourself harbor bigotry based in a suspicion that women might be inferior, you might simply ask a female friend to enlighten you.

And as to those who still are playing sixties-era feminism's strident tune, for the sake of the world please make a point of learning to overcome your remaining bigotry against anyone you imagine still oppresses you. The fight for the principle of female equality has decisively been won in the United States (Thank you!), so it is time now to shift our attention toward intense cross-gender kindness and healing.

- **Democrats/Republicans or Left/Right.** Our most intractable form of bigotry other than the primary topic of this book is the insane political emotions that are now tearing this nation apart. Your authors enjoy friends of every political stripe, and we have found that they all are wonderful people who seem to be aligned in what they want for this country but they only disagree about the best ways to get there. We are confident that there are very few real racist-misogynist-homophobes now, and we are coming to see all this extreme left-right nonsense is nothing more than ignorant bigotry. We ask you please if you find yourself detesting everyone who opposes you politically to consider the possibility that it is you who are bigoted. You have the power now to dare to trust and begin to dialog with everyone; and for the sake of those who still are subject to racial bigotry in this country, we ask you please to make that effort!

Helping others to overcome their bigotry is a matter of treating them with kindness, patience, and respect, no matter what they do. The first moment when you call someone a racist, or when you even imply the epithet, you are closing one more mind to new ideas and perhaps you are creating a racist for life. Each time you do this you are making it harder for us to end America's racial problems, so please do not do it ever again! Instead, share your own experiences, encourage each small opening of your bigoted friends to new ideas, and help us all to hasten the day when every American has overcome a reflexive need to pass judgments on other people.

For yourself, if you have uncomfortable feelings about others that might be bigotry, we urge you to read and try the non-religious teachings of Jesus in Appendix III. It turns out that Jesus really knew what he was talking about, and he gave us the easiest and most effective method for overcoming our bigotry that you can imagine.

So now it is your turn to think about what you might do to help to build a better tomorrow. Each American is going to be instrumental in changing the climate of this nation away from its present combative roughness and toward the universal love for others that is going to be essential if we are ever to return our country to its position as a shining city on a hill, with its founding principles of freedom and equality still the best hope of humankind.

Chapter Nine
The Crucial Role of Individual Action

"Every great dream begins with a dreamer. Always remember, you have within you the strength, the patience, and the passion to reach for the stars to change the world."

—Harriet Tubman, American abolitionist and Civil War hero (1822–1913)

"Every man must decide whether he will walk in the light of creative altruism or in the darkness of destructive selfishness."

—Martin Luther King, Jr., winner of the 1964 Nobel Peace Prize (1929–1968)

"A president can ask for reconciliation in the racial conflict that divides Americans. But reconciliation comes only from the hearts of people."

—Richard Nixon, 37th president of the United States (1913–1994)

"There are those who look at things the way they are, and ask why . . . I dream of things that never were, and ask why not?"

—Robert F. Kennedy, American Senator (1925–1968)

"For all sad words of tongue and pen, the saddest are these, 'It might have been'."

—John Greenleaf Whittier, American poet and abolitionist (1807–1892)

"We must, indeed, all hang together or, most assuredly, we shall all hang separately."

—Benjamin Franklin, American Founding Father (1706–1790)

If you are feeling the way many before us have felt— that it is time at last to heal our Civil War wounds— you will find that you have resources and options that Americans never have had before. The most important, of course, is that now we have conclusively proven that many possible solutions will not work. No point in trying any of that again! And fifty years after The Civil Rights Act of 1964, we also have the benefit of many more melanin-blessed Americans who have achieved the middle class and are prepared to lend their insights as we work to get this done for those who haven't managed to make the same leap. I recall that while this nation was in the midst of freedom marches and bus boycotts, many people had the awful sense that never again would we know racial peace; but fifty years on, we can reasonably hope that racial strife can now be put forever behind us.

In some ways, though, we are breaking new ground, and for that we are going to need a new mindset that is calmer, gentler, and more loving. Here are some essential rules by which we all must now abide:

- **Be careful not to offend people whose present understanding might be limited.** If someone says something that you think sounds bigoted, where once you might have snapped that she was being a racist, now you must just say something mild like, "My goodness, do you really think so?" If you know from prior encounters that someone of your acquaintance has formed bigoted views, then gently share a few positive stories and perhaps introduce somebody nice who happens to have the targeted shade of skin. But never attempt to confront your apparently bigoted friend or family member about race! If he confronts you anyway, apologize and withdraw and then seek a future chance to gently share new ideas. It's a lot more work to open people's minds than it is to dismiss them from your life, but each person whose mind you manage to touch will be one less obstacle on this nation's road to joyous racial unity.

- **Never take sides.** In this work of healing our nation, there are no sides! Your melanin-enriched friend who says nasty things about white people is every bit as much in the wrong as is your white friend who uses the N-word. You should not right- out confront your friend, but if you keep forever in mind your need never to take sides between the races then you can just look for every chance to gently open all the bigoted minds around you.
- **Give people a wonderful reputation to live up to.** This is an old Dale Carnegie trick, and it works amazingly well. Even with the most evil-seeming people, find one thing about them that you can praise and then praise it. If your curmudgeonly uncle says something awful about those of a skin color he does not share, you might mildly tell him that you disagree, or you just might not say anything. But soon thereafter, find occasion to say, "You're so nice to have me at your house today. Would you like to play Scrabble? You're great at that!" Or, "You take such good care of your dogs, Uncle Jeb. I want to come back as one of them!" Helping people to feel good about themselves is the most effective way

there is to help them begin to feel better about even the different-seeming people that they once disdained.
- **Fight wrongdoing with love.** The greatest American of the twentieth century was Martin Luther King, Jr. He could have been just one more rabble-rouser, ranting against injustices and shouting threats, but instead he spoke words of powerful inspiration and he led his fight wielding only love. He won those first battles. He knew that the path of nonviolence and reconciliation was the only way that he could have won them! May each of us keep our beloved friend Martin's constant example in our hearts. With his help we now will together finish the work that he so well began.

This need always to put love first will mean that you never can join a racial cause or a demonstration unless it follows Dr. King's example. There are many melanin-blessed bigots, too, and especially if the belated efforts being made now to complete emancipation begin to seem politically controversial, those of us working to make it happen might find ourselves being attacked from all sides. If you had no touchstone but your zeal to right wrongs, you might become caught up in doing something angry; but if you will keep the above list of imperatives always foremost in your mind, and our beloved Martin strong in your heart, then you will steer a steady course.

And if most of your friends look a lot like you, then you ought to go out and make some new friends! Take a course at a local college, spend time in a mixed-race church, do some civic work, or if you have a mixed-race kind of hobby join a special-interest group. Even reach out to pastors of both racial persuasions and ask them to join you in starting a mixed-race social Meetup. Then never talk about race! Instead, find people with whom you click and spend some time with them. Make couples-friends and get your children together for play-dates. You and they may feel self-conscious at first, but surprisingly soon you are going to see your new friends for themselves and not for their skin shades. If enough Americans will do this, we can begin at once to blur racial lines until soon there will be no race left in America but the human race.

Finally, please never forget that every good result is a great result, no matter who helps to bring it forth. Even if you did not vote for him, if President Trump takes advantage of his historic opportunity and leads us to complete emancipation, then please thank him and bless him for it. Waiting another four years, or eight years, or twelve, until we have whatever president you might prefer, will only unnecessarily blight the lives of even more millions of precious children.

Chapter Ten
Envisioning a United Country and an Eternally Peaceful World

"In America, with all of its evils and faults, you can still reach through the forest and see the sun. But we don't know yet whether that sun is rising or setting for our country."
—Dick Gregory, American civil rights activist, comedian, and entrepreneur

"Change will not come if we wait for some other person or some other time. We are the ones we've been waiting for. We are the change that we seek."
—Barack Obama, 44th president of the United States

"My dream is of a place and a time where America will once again be seen as the last best hope of earth."
—Abraham Lincoln, 16th president of the United States (1809–1865)

"Whatever America hopes to bring to pass in the world must first come to pass in the heart of America."
—Dwight Eisenhower, 34th president of the United States (1890–1969)

"No other country in the world does what we do. On every issue, the world turns to us, not simply because of the size of our economy or our military might—but because of the ideals we stand for, and the burdens we bear to advance them."
—Barack Obama, 44th president of the United States

"When I am president, I will work to ensure that all of our kids are treated equally and protected equally. Every action I take, I will ask myself, 'Does this make life better for young Americans in Baltimore, Chicago, Detroit, Ferguson, who have as much of a right to live out their dreams as any other child in America?'"
—Donald Trump, 45th president of the United States

This world has been in chaos for a hundred years, to the point where world chaos now seems normal. We cannot imagine a peaceful world in which countries live together as neighbors, in which we trade freely and offer help when needed and no child suffers want. Your authors understand how difficult it is for you to imagine that better world, but here, too, we can look for insights by gaming out a different history.

Imagining a World Led by a More Powerful America

There were occasional wars before 1914, but we called World War I "the Great War" for a reason! For the first time, much of the world's population was lined up on one side or another of a bloody and climactic war in which more than seventeen million people died. There were thirty-eight million killed or wounded, and the number of people whose lives were blighted is beyond all human calculation. Then World War I led to World War II in ways that in hindsight should have been foreseeable, and for decades thereafter we lived an active "cold war" that cost us trillions in munitions build-up, in lost trade, and in the distractions and general sapping of energy that low-grade terror will induce. Then came Vietnam and wars in the Middle East. No one living can remember a peaceful world.

So it is time for one more thought-experiment. What might the past century have looked like globally if a young America had managed to pull that rock from beneath the sapling of liberty so it always could have grown straight and true?

Let's assume that complete emancipation occurs in America by 1870. Either Martha Jefferson survives her illness and she and Thomas make it happen before 1820, or a wiser Congress begins about then a program of public education that enables President

Lincoln to sign the Full Emancipation Act of 1861. By 1866, every slave has been freed and the process of education and empowerment has begun. So then by 1890 emancipation is almost a generation into the past, and the impact of so many productive people entering the burgeoning middle class is producing an economic boom in America like nothing the world has ever seen. The America that enters the twentieth century has never suffered a civil war, and it is united and healthy and incredibly rich.

What happens now will be a pattern for the century to come.

The squabbles between European nations that have been going on since time out of mind are still hanging over from the nineteenth century, all the border fusses and the forming and breaking and forming again of alliances, so the outbreak of World War I is the unplanned result of just more regional nonsense. Perhaps we are unable to prevent the war's outbreak, but a rich and healthy America that has felt no need to form foreign alliances is able to avoid being drawn into it. At first it stays out altogether, speaking softly and carrying a big stick (in President Teddy Roosevelt's memorable phrase), waiting for those involved to come to their senses. Then as the war escalates, a mild threat is made that we will come over there and knock some heads unless everyone agrees to come to the table, and we couple our threat with a promise that when the shooting ends we will ensure the peace. It is impossible to read a history of that war without seeing ways that it might have been ended before it nearly ended civilization, and a much more powerful America that never had been blighted by its Civil War could have played a crucial mediating and enforcement role.

After World War I, the stage is set to begin a century of peace.

Even if it has felt forced to enter the Great War as a combatant, a much more powerful United States is able to force an end to that war, and to shape its ending in the gracious and bountiful way in which America ends its wars. From the efforts made after the Civil War to bring this country back together right through the compassion that we showed to the people of Japan and Germany after World War II, we try to help and heal those that we vanquish. Americans are simply like that.

So as we envision this different reality, we see America presiding over a love-fest in the aftermath of World War I. A compassionate rather than a punitive ending to that war is able to rebuild all of Europe, and it prevents the German grievances that otherwise could have led to the rise of a vindictive monster like Adolph Hitler. And . . . well, you can take it from there.

It seems to us reasonable to assume that a healthy America could have led the world through an altogether peaceful and prosperous twentieth century. No Second World War, no Holocaust, no need to establish Israel as a refugee state, no cold war, and if we were powerful enough and sensible enough to always lead the world wisely then perhaps not ever any wars at all. Realizing what a giant this country would have been without the Civil War and slavery's long tail, we think the world is fortunate indeed that the United States matured into power after all the big empire-building games had been played! In every war that we have fought, all that this nation ever has kept has been the land needed to bury its dead.

As you play out the past century of world history for yourself, you will realize what a gigantic tragedy it has been for everyone on earth that this country was unable to free its slaves before it fought its ineffective and disastrous Civil War. And we note, not entirely in jest, that Martha Jefferson's untimely death may have been the most consequential event in the history of the world since the birth of Jesus! Playing out the better series of world events that could have followed Thomas Jefferson's complete emancipation early in the nineteenth century, right through dynamic national growth with never any of the terrible costs of keeping thirteen percent of Americans in servitude, that peaceful world led by the United States is even less recognizable to us now than is a slavery-free America. The leadership of a wise and benevolent titan centered on a healthy tree of liberty for all of the past two centuries could have put this world a thousand years ahead of where it is today!

So then the question sadly becomes whether such a stable and glorious future for every human being on earth still is possible. Without the leadership of a healthy United States, there doesn't seem to be much hope that we ever can end all these terrible conflicts and the naked tyranny of regional powers. What other nation has the strength or the will to finally lead this world past fighting? In this, as in its hopeful example of individual freedom and empowerment, the United States truly is the world's best hope.

It is 1790. That clever young Jefferson who lately penned the Declaration of Independence has been talking up a storm in Virginia about the need that he sees to end slavery now so our tree of liberty can grow straight and true. He is circulating pamphlets to all the state capitals on the added efficiencies of farming with free labor. He writes often about how well his slaves are doing on their own small farms, while his abolitionist wife writes broadsides to demonstrate how the children of slaveholders are brutalized by their exposure to slavery. Together they paint a terrible picture of all the ways in which slavery might otherwise blight this nation in a hundred years, or even in two hundred years, if we don't find a way to end it now. And Americans are beginning to listen. . . .

We cannot change anything about the past. We are sure that Americans would have done a lot more to end slavery long ago if they could have foreseen the mess that they would otherwise be bequeathing to us, but we cannot blame them for things not done. And now the present belongs to us, with all its imperfections and all its possibilities.

The real question is: How will we shape the future?

Appendices

Appendix I
Reading Suggestions

Most of what has been written about our racial problems is angry. Often it assigns blame. While such negativity may be justified, it cannot be of any use to us now, so instead here is a brief reading list that is meant to reconnect you with America's founding ideals and to offer resources that might be of assistance as we work together to get beyond the burden of exhaustion and pain that each American still carries from our battle with slavery's long tail.

Founding Documents

The foremost American thinkers of the eighteenth, nineteenth, and twentieth centuries have left us three core expressions of the great human ideal that is America. Their dream is the American dream! And it still is not too late for us to work together to make their dream come true.

The Declaration of Independence (1776)

If there is any one expression of what it means to be an American, it is the first two paragraphs of this Declaration that was signed as the thirteen colonies began their separation from Britain. It was produced by a committee, but its author and the source of its energy was 33-year-old Thomas Jefferson.

Money quote: **"We hold these truths to be self-evident, that all men are created equal, that they are endowed by their Creator with certain unalienable Rights, that among these are Life, Liberty and the pursuit of Happiness.—That to secure these** rights, Governments are instituted among Men, deriving their just powers from the consent of the governed." These words continue to express the perfect ideal that is America. And they wait, even today, for Americans at last to fully grow into all that we can be.

The Gettysburg Address (1863)

During the worst moments of the Civil War, President Abraham Lincoln helped to dedicate the cemetery that held the more than seven thousand casualties of the Battle of Gettysburg. Its money quote is the entire speech:

"Four score and seven years ago our fathers brought forth upon this continent a new nation, conceived in liberty and dedicated to the proposition that 'all men are created equal.'

"Now we are engaged in a great civil war, testing whether that nation, or any nation so conceived and so dedicated, can long endure. We are met on a great battlefield of that war. We have come to dedicate a portion of it as a final resting place for those who died here, that the nation might live. This we may, in all propriety, do. But, in a larger sense, we cannot dedicate—we cannot consecrate—we cannot hallow this ground. The brave men, living and dead, who struggled here have hallowed it far above our poor power to add or detract. The world will little note nor long remember what we say here; while it can never forget what they did here.

"It is rather for us, the living, to be here dedicated to the great task remaining before us—that from these honored dead we take increased devotion to that cause for which they here gave their last full measure of devotion. That we here highly resolve these dead shall not have died in vain; that this nation shall have a new birth of freedom, and that government of the people, by the people, for the people shall not perish from the earth."

The fact that the American Civil War was an almost unmitigated disaster for the nation, and especially for the legally freed slaves and for their descendants even to this day, can take nothing away from the purity of that moment when the 16th President of the United States carried forward the perfect sentiment that the 3rd President had first expressed for us when he was very young.

Letter from Birmingham Jail (1963)

Martin Luther King, Jr., was a phenomenal human being. That he was the greatest American of the twentieth century is certain by now; what still is in contention is whether anyone who was living then has earned a near second place. We urge you to read his words and study his life, and we especially hope that you will read this masterpiece. It will express for you more clearly than we ever could what it felt like to be still struggling for freedom and for basic human dignity a full century after legal emancipation.

A few money quotes:

"Injustice anywhere is a threat to justice everywhere. We are caught in an inescapable network of mutuality, tied in a single garment of destiny. Whatever affects one directly, affects all indirectly."

"Lamentably, it is an historical fact that privileged groups seldom give up their privileges voluntarily. Individuals may see the moral light and voluntarily give up their unjust posture; but, as Reinhold Niebuhr has reminded us, groups tend to be more immoral than individuals. We know through painful experience that freedom is never voluntarily given by the oppressor; it must be demanded by the oppressed."

"For years now I have heard the word 'Wait!' It rings in the ear of every Negro with piercing familiarity. This 'Wait' has almost always meant 'Never.' We must come to see, with one of our distinguished jurists, that 'justice too long delayed is justice denied.' We have waited for more than 340 years for our constitutional and God given rights."

And finally, there is this wrenching plea. Recall that it was written a full hundred years almost to the day after the Emancipation Proclamation was signed, and as you read it you will weep.

"Perhaps it is easy for those who have never felt the stinging darts of segregation to say, 'Wait.' But when you have seen vicious mobs lynch your mothers and fathers at will and drown your sisters and brothers at whim; when you have seen hate filled policemen curse, kick and even kill your black brothers and sisters; when you see the vast majority of your twenty million Negro brothers smothering in an airtight cage of poverty in the midst of an affluent society; when you suddenly find your tongue twisted and your speech stammering as you seek to explain to your six year old daughter why she can't go to the public amusement park that has just been advertised on television, and see tears welling up in her eyes when she is told that Funtown is closed to colored children, and see ominous clouds of inferiority beginning to form in her little mental sky, and see her beginning to distort her personality by developing an unconscious bitterness toward white people; when you have to concoct an answer for a five year old son who is asking: 'Daddy, why do white people treat colored people so mean?'; when you take a cross county drive and find it necessary to sleep night after night in the uncomfortable corners of your automobile because no motel will accept you; when you are humiliated day in and day out by nagging signs reading 'white' and 'colored'; when your first name becomes 'nigger,' your middle name becomes 'boy' (however old you are) and your last name becomes 'John,' and your wife and mother are never given the respected title 'Mrs.'; when you are harried by day and haunted by night by the fact that you are a Negro, living constantly at tiptoe stance, never quite knowing what to expect next, and are plagued with inner fears and outer resentments; when you are forever fighting a degenerating sense of 'nobodiness'—then you will understand why we find it difficult to wait."

Martin Luther King, Jr. wrote this letter at the age of 34. He may in fact have been the greatest human being who ever lived.

Our Personal Recommendations

Exodus: From the Door of No Return – Roy G. Phillips (2006) — This book by Kelley Glover's father describes the story of his family as it journeyed through slavery, Reconstruction, Jim Crow segregation, the great migration out of the south, the World Wars, the Civil Rights Movement, and the tumultuous period of the sixties and seventies through to the dawning of the 21st century. It is the story of how the author and his family rose and evolved amid the storms of racism by means of dedication, discipline, determination, and hard work. Roberta wants you to know that when at last Dr. Phillips goes back to that doorway from which his ancestors embarked long ago, and he falls to his knees, there will be tears on your cheeks.

My Thomas – Roberta Grimes (1993, 2015) — Most attempts to understand Thomas Jefferson are overviews of the great man that he became, and many include a political lie as if it were a likely fact. This book, which may be an autobiography, is a wonderful American love story and a front-row seat on the American Revolution. We wish Roberta's name were not on it! We invite you to read it anyway.

Kelley's Four Guides to the Healing and Transformational Power of Agape Love

The Mastery of Love – Don Miguel Ruiz (1999) — In this text, Don Miguel Ruiz explains the Toltec perspective on love. In answer to the question of what love really is, he highlights the misplaced expectations that permeate most relationships.

Spiritual Liberation – Michael Bernard Beckwith (2009)— Michael Beckwith teaches that inner spiritual work, not religiosity or dogma, liberates us. He draws on a wide spectrum of ancient wisdom teachers such as Jesus the Christ and Gautama the Buddha; contemporary spiritual luminaries like Thich Nhat Hanh, Sri Aurobindo, and the Dalai Lama; and Western contributors to the New Thought tradition of spirituality such as Emanuel Swedenborg, Walter Russell, and Dr. Howard Thurman to create a profound new belief synthesis.

The Imprint Journey – Liliane Desjardins (2011) — We all have imprints, both negative and positive. An imprint is a belief that shapes our thoughts and actions, a belief that we often hold unconsciously. Liliane Desjardins, a certified clinical addiction specialist, who is co-founder of Pavillon Gilles Desjardins and co-creator of the Desjardins Unified Model of Treatment of Addictions, sets forth in this book an exploration of imprints, how they govern our lives, and how we can reprogram our minds to function in new and fulfilling ways.

Breaking the Habit of Being Yourself – Dr. Joe Dispenza (2013) — You are not doomed by your genes and hardwired to be a certain way for the rest of your life! A new science is emerging that empowers all human beings to create the reality they choose. This renowned author, speaker, researcher, and chiropractor combines the fields of quantum physics, neuroscience, brain chemistry, biology, and genetics to show you what is possible.

Roberta's Guide to Personal Transformation Using the Teachings of Jesus

The Fun of Growing Forever – Roberta Grimes (2016) — The Gospel teachings turn out to be the simplest and most effective program for spiritual growth and personal empowerment that ever has been designed. Again, our apologies for Roberta's name on this book! The true Author is not a religious figure, but he is instead a phenomenal Teacher who today is speaking to us all. **Had we not felt the historical urgency of this moment, we would have delayed this book for a year and come up with further reading recommendations.** We plan to undertake that search now, and will include more suggestions in a later edition. Meanwhile, if you have found books on the topic of racial healing that you believe will be helpful to others, we invite you to suggest them to us through the contact block at robertagrimes.com.

Appendix II
Kelley's Transformational Healing Tool

Heart Coherence Breathing
Kelley Glover

"Your task is not to seek love, but merely to seek and find all the barriers within yourself that you have built against it."

—Rumi, 13th century mystic poet

*I*t is my belief that we are here as human beings to help each other remember who we are. And when I say remember, I mean *re*-member. We give each other so many tools of destruction so we can *dis*-member ourselves that we forget that we are all on this spiritual journey to help each other to *re*-member our wholeness, and to literally help put each other back together again. Separation is merely an illusion. We are all one with the One. I truly believe that is my soul's purpose. To remember my greatness, and to remind others of their greatness, too. It all begins within. That is where the shift happens. Within. Pointing fingers at others and scribbling in other people's coloring books instead of focusing on your *own* coloring book of life is what causes fear, mistrust, anger, and ultimately a collective consciousness of suffering. The buck stops with *you!*

So, where do you begin?

I went on a spiritual retreat back in 2008 with two counselors named Liliane and Gilles Desjardins. During their four-day retreat, we did a lot of personal inventory work and I learned how family imprints shape how we perceive ourselves in relation to others as we navigate through this spiritual journey called our lives. Most recently, I worked with Caroline Eick, the daughter of Liliane DesJardins, and discovered how emotions can get stuck in the body and cause all sorts of physical pain and mental instability if we identify ourselves as our emotions. I am here to tell you that we are *not* our emotions. Emotions are merely indicators of how we are feeling. In order for us as emotional beings to live mentally and physically healthier lives, we must learn how to allow negative emotions to move *through* our bodies. When our identity becomes our emotions, those emotions get stuck within our physical bodies and can cause physical pain, mental anguish, and actual addiction to suffering. When we allow emotions to act as merely indicators, and we become the observer of those emotions, they can instead be our friends and can help us to grow into more spiritually mature beings.

Believing the negative stories we make up in our minds about ourselves and each other is where bigotry and intolerance begins. Bigotry, and all the emotions associated with it including fear and mistrust, become stuck pattern in our minds that loop in our thought patterns over and over again. These stuck, negative thought patterns are where diseased thinking lives. It is up to us as individuals to learn how to interrupt and break negative, diseased thought patterns that harm us and harm those around us. We have the power to actually change our own body chemistry. We can shift and change our thought patterns without the use of drugs!

Heart-Mind Coherence Breathing

Here is a tool that I learned from Caroline Eick of the Center for Heart-Mind Coherence. When you are feeling a negative emotion such as anger, for example, try the following:

Be aware of the anger. Slowly inhale this thought: **"I accept that I am feeling angry."** As you exhale, exhale the following thought, focusing that exhale from your heart, **"I Am Peace."** Repeat this process seven times. Slowly inhale your acceptance that you *feel* the negative emotion, and then slowly exhale the opposite, *positive* emotion and the thought, **"I Am Peace."** Focus your energy so you feel that you actually are exhaling from your heart. When you repeat this process seven times (seven heart-coherent breaths), one of two things will happen:

1. The emotion will dissipate as the body releases it, causing a shift in your emotion to create healthier brain waves and heart beats per minute; or
2. Another emotion will try to move in with the anger, and/or the anger will just not leave.

If the latter happens, ask the anger what it has to say to you, and listen. Actually say to yourself, **"Anger, what do you have for me? What do you want to say to me?"** Either it will go away, or it will drop some wisdom onto your plate! Write down what the anger has to say to you. When I do that, some really wise, introspective things come out on the page. And the negative emotions will finally go away.

Doing this practice daily will help you reach a place of "Agape" love. Agape love, the highest level of love, is "an energy that creates, heals, transforms, attracts, blesses, prospers, and is unconditional," as Lilane Desjardins puts it!

To further understand the healing power of Agape Love, and a way to transform your mind and your body, I recommend four books listed in Appendix I as a starting point. I also *highly* recommend the practice of meditation for at least twenty minutes a day! You will be surprised at how your life will begin to shift in so many wondrous ways when you reconnect with Source every day. Even if you are an atheist and you do not believe in a concept of God, I know that meditation will work for you. The simple act of slow inhale and slow exhale and allowing your thoughts to just drift by like clouds across the sky while you don't attach yourself to those thoughts is all that you need. Start with five minutes, and work your way up to twenty minutes a day. Just being aware of your breathing is enough!

"If you want to make the world a better place, take a look at yourself and make that change!"

—Siedah Garrett and Glen Ballard

Appendix III
Roberta's Transformational Healing Tool

The Universal Forgiveness that Jesus Taught
Roberta Grimes

Of the two core spiritual practices that Jesus teaches in the Gospels, forgiveness is the one that we have trouble learning. Yet learning how to forgive perfectly must come before we can learn how to love! It is not an exaggeration to say that until you have mastered universal forgiveness, you won't be able even to fathom what it means to love as Jesus taught us to love, in a manner that actually transforms us internally.

What's more, forgiveness is about a lot more than just getting over our personal grudges. Forgiveness is the method by which we release every barrier to our awareness of love's presence. It banishes fear, anger, mistrust, self-doubt, prejudices and bigotry, and every other negative thought. Forgiveness creates for you the peace within that will allow you to let things be.

My husband has been meditating daily for more than forty years. Kelley also meditates. I have other friends who meditate, too, and everyone tells me how well it works, but I don't have the patience for meditation. And twenty minutes out of every day is a hundred and twenty hours of each year! With so much essential work to do now, who really has the time for that?

Fortunately, there is a very much easier, while-you're-walking-around sort of way to achieve a similar peaceful result. If you will faithfully do the following exercise whenever anything bothers you at all, within a month or two you will find that you need to do it much less often. And if you remain vigilant about going back to it whenever you seem to be starting to slip, soon you will have the comfort of realizing that nothing much ever will bother you again.

This is a mind-trick. The reason why it works so well is that our minds are not the efficient computers that we like to imagine them to be, but rather they are:

- **Lazy.** Our minds establish emotional links as simple reactions that begin with any sort of stimulus. We begin to form these stimulus- reaction links in infancy, and often we have no idea what the reason is that we react to stimuli as we do. For example, we might fear black poodles because when we were eighteen months old some black poodle snarled at us.
- **Habitual.** We believe that we are always thinking! But in fact, we do little active thinking, since if we had to pause and think through opening a door or putting on a shoe or composing a sentence or steering a car each time we did even basic things we would have to spend our days that way and we'd have little time for anything else.
- **Highly Adaptable.** Fortunately, the fact that our minds are both lazy and habitual can be used to our advantage. The links that we've established are only what our minds have perceived to be the easiest path; but if we interrupt those links and present to our minds an easier way forward, they will take the new way.

Think of water flowing in a rocky stream. When we move a few rocks, the water at once flows differently.

Overcoming old emotional reactions isn't quite this simple, but it's close. We tend to build up justifications in our minds for our emotional reactions to things, so in the case of black poodles we might develop a certainty that we read somewhere a few years back that the color black in poodles is genetically linked to aggression. Depending upon our personalities, these memories (many of which are false) of reasons for our bigoted views might make it more difficult to reconfigure our minds; but that blessed combination of laziness and adaptability makes reprogramming our minds still pretty easy.

You can use the following technique to get over—or to forgive—your reaction to any kind of stimulus at all, but let's assume here that you have an aversion to anyone with a different shade of skin. It's a visceral reaction. You think it happens because in the third grade someone was cruel to you on a playground, or because you once lived in a mixed-race neighborhood and someone who lived there and looked different from your family used to tease you. Or they stole your mail. It doesn't matter why you believe that you reasonably have come to feel as you do, and it doesn't even matter if the feeling is justified: for the sake of the country you love and for the sake of the future of the world, you have decided that it is time to get rid of it.

Applying radical forgiveness to negative emotional reactions to people is easy. Beginning today, whenever you notice someone who is likely to spark a negative reaction in you, simply stop what you are doing and spread your arms wide and use them to mentally gather up that person, all your feelings about that person and about everyone else who might look like that person, and even each thing that you imagine that people who look that way have seemed to you to do wrong, and together with all the negative emotions that you might be feeling as you do this gathering, form it all up into a nice, tight ball. Really tamp it down small with your hands! It can be good to recognize your own complicity in having ever nurtured these negative feelings, and mentally jump into that ball as well. Use your whole arms to do this, and really make a show for yourself of forming that ball, since the more physical you are, the more your mind will be influenced. Then vigorously push that ball away with both hands as you say, **"I love you, I bless you, I forgive, and I release."** And always, always mean it.

If you like, you even might do it twice, especially in the beginning. And don't worry that doing it in public will make you feel stupid. You are reprogramming your mind to stop reacting to the sight of someone with that other shade of skin; and the more your mind hates doing this exercise, the easier it will be for you to get it to stop reacting.

If you are firm about this, and always take time to form the ball while thinking about who and what you are putting into it, and then you push it away while saying aloud (or at least thinking) the forgiveness mantra, **"I love you, I bless you, I forgive, and I release,"** you should find that after a month or two something interesting is happening. Don't look for it! Simply do the exercise every time you face a potential stimulus. But one day, oddly, you will realize that someone with the wrong shade of skin actually has looked at you crankily, and you no longer care. At one time, that look from him would have driven you right up the wall! But now you hardly shrug. No emotional reaction.

The closest analogy I can give to describe the difference this makes in your mind is maybe something like the concept of levers.

You used to have levers on the outside that people could fiddle with and get a reaction, but now those levers have been disconnected on the inside. People still will fiddle with them, but now they cannot affect you. It's a new softness, a deep internal quietness that makes your mind feel like a safer and more beautiful place.

When you insist that your mind not strongly react to something that used to set you off, it turns out that your mind is sufficiently lazy that your no longer reacting negatively whenever it offers up that old stimulus will cause it pretty soon to stop trying. Now it has a new habit, it no longer reacts, and this new, easier way for your mind to flow becomes its new normal. It really is that easy! So long as you always are careful to form and forgive that ball if your mind ever again shows any sign of going back to its old reaction, you have created for yourself a more peaceful and positive reality for the rest of your life.

If you are interested in further exploring this and other spiritual teachings of Jesus in a simple, positive, and non- religious way, you might check out *The Fun of Growing Forever* in Appendix I.

Appendix IV
What Would Jesus Really Do?

Roberta Grimes

*A*mong *the biggest problems that Americans face in attempting to come together as a nation is the fact that so many of us are Christians.* By grace of the wisdom of our Founding Fathers, our freedom of religion is absolute! But, more and more, some of Christianity's teachings are proving to be divisive at a time when America so badly needs unity and healing. So if we love both our country and our Lord, you and I now face a conundrum. Let's talk about how we might start to resolve it.

Please understand that I am speaking here only to traditional Christians. If this isn't you, then you have many better things to do than to read this Appendix, so please go and do those things with my love. For Christians, let me first share with you my history as a sister in faith. After an experience of light at the age of eight (which was followed by a second at the age of 20), I began in my teens to read the entire Christian Bible from cover to cover repeatedly, every day, and I kept that up into my fifties. I majored in early Christian history in college. I expected to become a minister. Then I fell in love with and married a Catholic, so I was an ardent Catholic for twenty-five years.

I won't argue with your religious beliefs. You ought to believe whatever speaks to your heart! I just want you to understand that:

- **The Christian Bible is internally inconsistent.** It's an historical document, parts of which directly contradict other important parts. If you don't believe me, please do what I have done, and sit down and actually read the whole Book.

- **There is no independent evidence that every word of the Bible comes from God.** Understanding that fact was a relief to me, given how bad some of it is! The notion that the entire Bible is the Inspired Word of God comes from the Council of Nicaea, which was held in the year 325. I have studied the Council of Nicaea. If you think the whole Bible is God's Word, then I urge you to do the same. Just be warned: if you love hot dogs, you will not want to watch them being made!

- **The Gospel words of Jesus should come first for Christians.** Many clergymen seem to think it's fine to use the Old Testament or the balance of the New Testament to modify—or even to replace—the pure and uncompromising words of the Lord. But the Gospels are the only place where Jesus teaches us directly, and nowhere in those four books does He suggest that it is fine to use other teachings to modify His own! Indeed, He says precisely the opposite. Jesus is the Reason for the Season. If we really are His followers, then His truth is the first and the last, the Alpha and the Omega. And His truth is plainly stated in His Gospel teachings.

- **The Council of Nicaea even edited the Gospels.** They removed some of what Jesus had been heard to say, and they added some passages about ideas then in vogue, especially including End Times prophesy and church-building. It turns out to be pretty easy to spot what the Council must have added, and unless you relegate those added words to second-tier status you cannot live the Lord's truth.

With these four caveats in mind, let's look at how the Gospels tell us that Jesus would want us to act today. This is a study that you can undertake yourself on all kinds of topics, but for our purpose we'll be apply the Gospel teachings just to the problem of bigotry against other people. Some Christians hold bigoted views of other Christians, but the real bigotry in nearly all Christian denominations is against practicing homosexuals.

My observation has been that Christians can be amazingly judgmental! And this is ironic, given Jesus's big directive that we must not judge. He said, **"Do not judge, or you too will be judged. For in the same way you judge others, you will be judged, and with the measure you use, it will be measured to you. Why do you look at the speck of sawdust in your brother's eye and pay no attention to the plank in your own eye? How can you say to your brother, 'Let me take the speck out of your eye,' when all the time there is a plank in your own eye? You hypocrite, first take the plank out of your own eye, and then you will see clearly to remove the speck from your brother's eye."** (MT 7:1–5) So in fact, whenever you and I judge anyone for anything we are directly disobeying Jesus!

Yes, but wait! What about, **"If there is a man who lies with a male as those who lie with a woman, both of them have committed a detestable act; they shall surely be put to death. Their blood guiltiness is upon them."** (LV 20:13) True, but there is also, **"You shall not hate your fellow countryman in your heart; you may surely reprove your neighbor, but shall not incur sin because of him. You shall not take vengeance, nor bear any** grudge against the sons of your people, but you shall love your neighbor as yourself; I am the Lord." (LV 19:17–18)

And anyway, seizing on just that one Old Testament rule against homosexual practice and applying it strictly to other people is wrong when the Old Testament gives us many similar commands that no Christian follows. For example, if a girl is taken to wife and found to be not a virgin, **"then they shall bring out the girl to the doorway of her father's house, and the men of her city shall stone her to death."** (DT 22:21) If a son is rebellious and resists correction, **"then his father and mother shall seize him, and bring him out to the elders of his city at the gateway of his hometown. They shall say to the elders of his city, 'This son of ours is stubborn and rebellious, he will not obey us, he is a glutton and a drunkard.' Then all the men of his city shall stone him to death."** (DT 21:19–21) And if someone breaks any of God's commandments, or even falls away from religion, **"then you shall bring out that man or that woman who has done this evil deed to your gates, that is, the man or the woman, and you shall stone them to death."** (DT 17:5) "Thus you shall not show pity: life for life, eye for eye, tooth for tooth, hand for hand, foot for foot." (DT 19:21)

For goodness sake, even *eating shellfish or pork* (DT 14:8–10), *wearing blended fabrics* (LV 19:19), or *cutting your hair or beard, shaving, or wearing a tattoo* (LV 19:26–28) is a detestable Old Testament crime! So no well-dressed and nicely coifed Christian lives as if he or she believes the entire Bible is God's Inspired Word. *And if a well-dressed and nicely coifed clergyman tells you to condemn homosexuals, you know that he is using that one Old Testament rule to judge and bludgeon other people while he declines to live by the Old Testament himself.*

Jesus socialized with tax collectors and prostitutes, who were the dregs of society in His day, and He insisted that we not resist evil people. He said, **"You have heard that it was said, 'Love your neighbor and hate your enemy.' But I tell you, love your enemies and pray for those who persecute you, that you may be children of your Father in heaven. He causes his sun to rise on the evil and the good, and sends rain on the righteous and the unrighteous. If you love those who love you, what reward will you get? Are not even the tax collectors doing that? And if you greet only your own people, what are you doing more than others? Do not even pagans do that? Be perfect, therefore, as your heavenly Father is perfect.** (MT 5:43–48)

Perfection in loving everyone might seem to be an impossible standard, but it is to that standard of perfect love that Jesus still calls His followers today!

As a practical matter, what does all of this mean for modern Christians? Here are my two takeaways where homosexuality is concerned:

- **"Do not judge, or you too will be judged."** (MT 7:1) *This* is what Jesus truly commands! Judging other people is not our job, and I urge you as a Christian now to rededicate yourself to the living Lord. Read His Gospel teachings on love and forgiveness until you know them by heart.
- **"Love your enemies and pray for those who persecute you."** (MT 5:44) At the very least, Jesus calls us now to follow His example! He dined with tax collectors. When did you last break bread with people you might otherwise have judged? When did your church last

invite in local homosexuals without a plan to convert them, but simply to shower them with love and kindness? Your right to religious freedom should protect you from being forced to violate the tenets of your faith, but we aren't talking about civil law here. *Where in the teachings of Jesus do you find justification for not baking a cake or arranging flowers for people, just because you disapprove of their sex lives?*

Dear friends, when you and I stop cutting our hair and beards and we give up eating shrimp and pork and wearing blended fabrics, then our singling out of just a few Biblical laws to be strictly enforced against other people will be seen by our fellow Americans to be less hypocritical. Still, I have a suspicion that even then the Lord's command that we must love everyone perfectly is going to apply. What do you think?

You know the tale of the Good Samaritan. Jesus really means what He says! He truly wants us to consider each gay person, each sexual sinner, each person that we heretofore might have judged to be just like that traveler who was set upon by robbers and left to die on the road. You and I are called by the Lord to be that good Samaritan who showed compassion and bound up that stranger's wounds and cared for him, no matter who he was. And above all, we are call upon never to judge him! *If we want to consider ourselves followers of Jesus, how can we in conscience not do what He asks?*

www.ingramcontent.com/pod-product-compliance
Lightning Source LLC
Chambersburg PA
CBHW050249120526
44590CB00016B/2283